JOURNEYS

Published by Sampad South Asian Arts
c/o mac, Cannon Hill Park, Birmingham, B12 9QH UK

First Edition 2010

This selection and edition ©sampad 2010

Copyright of individual contributions remains with authors
All rights reserved

ISBN 978-0-9565416-2-8

Cover design by davewalshcreative.co.uk

Printed by www.beamreachuk.co.uk

www.sampad.org.uk

Sampad is a registered charity no. 1088995

JOURNEYS

Edited by
Anne Cockitt and Kavita Walia, sampad

Published by sampad

Sampad is a dynamic South Asian arts organisation based in Birmingham, playing a significant role regionally and nationally in promoting the appreciation and practice of the arts orginating from India, Pakistan, Bangladesh and Sri Lanka. The word sampad means wealth in Sanskrit and the organisation translates this as cultural wealth to be shared as widely as possible.

sampad
south asian arts

Foreword

Journeys continues to be a great travel experience for us at sampad. Not the ordinary travelling we do every day or on holidays but one that transports us through imagination and remarkable creativity. This quite a lengthy project, running over eighteen months, connected us with over 500 writers from.19 countries. From Staffordshire to Kolkata, and from Australia to Nigeria, we were impressed with the quality, passion and zeal of so many writers. The difficult task of selecting the competition winners was undertaken by a most august and experienced group who brought their own wisdom to the project.

At sampad we are continually striving to profile creative people in the most appropriate ways and felt that a publication was the best way to bring our writers to public attention. **Journeys** also adds to our international portfolio of projects developing intercultural dialogues across communities. I heartily congratulate all the writers who participated in **Journeys** and acknowledge the excellence of the winners. I do hope the book will provide pleasant reading for you and your friends and look forward to future literary journeys that will connect us to you and the world.

Piali Ray, Director, sampad

A cash prize was awarded to the overall winner in each category.

These winners are:

~ Writers aged 8 – 15 ~

Rida Vaquas – *The News* (p38)

~ Writers aged 16 and over ~

Hema Raman – *Shadow Men* (p127)

Contents

~ Writers aged 8-15 ~

Adrija Bandyopadhyay	The Junction	2
Samriddha Basu	Journey Of Life	4
Madhubrata Bhattacharyya	Pleasant Meadows	6
Anirban Datta Gupta	The Journey of Amun-Den to the New Land	9
Ankita Gupta	A letter 'To Whom It May Concern'	11
Siddhartha Haldar	A Journey Through Space	14
Raahat Kaduji	Your Journey is Just Beginning	16
Kanishk Kanakia	Blackberry's Journey To The Moon	18
Nur Kose	Trip to Bangladesh	20
Rajashree Mahanty	A Different Journey	21
Mrittika Majumdar	My Journey To Your Land	22
Haala Marikar	Wonder Full Vehicle	24
Sarah Murphy	A Thousand Wing Beats Away	25
Aindrila Pal	The Sailing Spirit of Journeys	27
Priyanjana Pramanik	All the Difference	28
Anuradha Rao	A Journey Of Friendship	30
Amitrajit Sarkar	Sands of Time	32
Yu Ching Tan	The Travelling Fire	34
Rida Vaquas	Roots	36
	The News	38
Chua Jun Yan	A Propeller's Coo	40

~ *Writers aged 16 and over* ~

Sabrina Ahmad	*Rewind*	44
Sairah Akhtar	*Lost and Found*	45
Mir Mahfuz Ali	*When Bangladesh*	
	Floats in a Water-hyacinth	46
	Bangladesh Began in Rain	47
	I am not a Stranger to this World	48
	Nobody Told Me	50
Kavita Amarnani	*My Grandmother's Laugh*	51
Asim Anwer Ansari	*I Journey*	52
Ranjit Singh Bahia	*The Beginning*	53
Amrita Bandopadhyay	*Home Tonight*	54
Juhi Basoya	*She Travels*	55
	Compass Travels	56
Michael Brett	*Bangladesh, London*	57
	London-from Aqaba to Zem Zem	58
Arun Budhathoki	*A Farewell Note*	60
	A Train Journey	62
	Confession	63
Safia Chaudhary	*Before*	64
	Life and Myself	66
Pervin Chhapkhanawala	*What's in a Name?*	67
Kshama Chhapkhanawalla	*Musical Chairs*	68
Kashif Choudhry	*The Patriarch*	69
Sala Choudhury	*Same to Same*	70
Renita D'Silva	*Dreams of Home*	71
Salil Desai	*For Old Times' Sake*	72
Hartman de Souza	*Untitled*	74
Tamsin Evans	*Six O'clock Meeting*	75

Aftab Khan Farooqui	To Mehr 01 - The South of France	76
	Notes To Mehr 04 – The West End, London	77
Roxanne Firdos	Not the Silk Road	78
Arun Ganapathy	Journey in Search of HIM on a Summer's Evening	80
Farah Ghuznavi	The Homecoming	82
Atar Hadari	The Return	83
Sabah Hadi	One Day	84
Judith Huang	Atomicae	86
Skinder Hundal	Ancient Clouds	88
Salahdin Imam	Australia Dreaming	89
Sahna Iqbal	Desired Flavour	90
Farrah Jarral	Pilgrimage	91
Pravin Jeyaraj	Coffee with a Stranger	92
Adrian Johnson	Impshi, impshi! Jaldi, jaldi!	93
Rasagya Kabra	The River	94
Rahul Karmakar	The Sea	95
	Father	96
Eisha Karol	My Mother	97
Tanuja Karunarathne	Journey of So Called Life	98
Masud Khan	Finding Anjan	99
Usha Kishore	The Journey of a Lifetime	100
Deepa Kylasam Iyer	Tryst with Destiny	102
Hazel Larkin	Party in Mumbai	104
Sid Lassi	Puttar! (Child)	105
Zhi Xin Lee	The Naming of Absences	106
Mina Maisuria	Farishta (Angel)	107
Munize Manzur	From Zero Point	108
	Of Bags and Baggage	110
Tisa Muhaddes	In the Womb	111
Iffat Nawaz	Three	112
Sue Newton	Pyjama Party	113

Aayush Niroula	*Home By Way Of Genes*	*114*
Saira Nisa	*Universal Time Traveller*	*116*
Avishek Parui	*If on a Winter's Night 2 Travellers*	*118*
Sahera Parveen	*God in Silence*	*120*
Sonali Pattnaik	*Rerouting To Arrival*	*122*
Amendra Pokharel	*From Slingshot Days*	*124*
Hema Raman	*Lost Messages*	*126*
	Shadow Men	*127*
Mohan Raorane	*I to Infinite*	*128*
Denise Robertson	*Journey's End*	*130*
Bal Saini	*My Mother's Land*	*131*
	The Final Promise	*132*
Ujwala Samarth	*Curry Sauce: A Journey To And From The Recipe That Is India*	*133*
Jayani Senanayake	*Pimply Faced Teenagers*	*135*
	Colonial Residue	*136*
	Bullet Hole in my Memory	*138*
Shaheema Shaw	*"Madam, only Rs. 40 to Nowhere, Chennai!"*	*140*
Sadaf Saaz Siddiqi	*Something Within*	*141*
	At Last	*142*
Navkirat Sodhi	*By and By*	*144*
Rajan Soni	*The Smell of Ancestors*	*146*
Shagorika Talukder	*Birds of Paradise*	*148*
	Shadows on a Wall	*150*
Ephraim Tan	*Connecting Dots*	*152*
	Cliffside	*153*
	Time Always	*154*
Takbir Uddin	*Home*	*155*
	Journey to the Motherland	*156*
Richa Wahi	*The Honeymoon*	*158*
	Let's Jog	*160*

Writers aged 8 – 15

Adrija Bandyopadhyay
Kolkata, India
Age 13

The Junction

I was in a by-lane. I dragged my tired feet into a building to get some rest. I had just ascended some stairs and reached the landing when a cat suddenly came upon me from nowhere and rubbed its furry head against my legs. Just then a door opened.

"Pussy! Where are you? "

The girl who had uttered these words dropped the bowl of cat food and stared. I managed to utter 'water' before dropping to the floor.

"Oh dear! Please come in."

While I gulped down a glass of water she said, "I'm Annapurna. What's your name?"
"Kabir"
"Isn't there a terrorist on the loose, by that name?"

My heart skipped a beat "Yeah, I guess."
"What do you do?"

I never told anyone the story of my life but somehow I could tell her. I told her that I was born into an extremely poor family and had to work hard to earn a living. In spite of everything I was beaten up every night by my drunken father. She looked at me, with empathy in her eyes. Her kindness and tender words touched me deeply.

When I came out of her apartment my mind was in turmoil.

"From a very early age I have been taught how to kill. That was all my life was about. Yet now, at this junction, I want things to change."

With great determination I set out into the lane, lighted with the glow of the setting sun.

Samriddha Basu
Kolkata, India
Age 12

Journey of Life

The greatest journey begins, in the mother's womb,
Ending with the person, peaceful in his tomb.
In between, we keep travelling through,
Wherever we go, whatever we do.

As some great man once said,
Each person comes with a different fate,
But in the end, as equals they go,
Within life's little drama show.

Some come with a role, some with none;
But each person is a unique one.
They learn about life, its values,
And see the world, with its different hues.

A great person completes his role,
And succeeds in achieving life's goal.
He receives immeasurable fame,
All the world remembers his name.

Some achieve fame, some do not,
Satisfied with what they've got.
But everybody is destined to fall,
Submit to Death, the end of all.

Submitting to Death is like the bow
To the cheering crowd at the end of the show.
The journey of life comes to a stop.
The end is nigh, the curtains drop.

The end of the journey, the end of the roads,
The end of all life's episodes.
The way to the end is always this
And you shall achieve the ultimate bliss.

Madhubrata Bhattacharyya
Kolkata, India
Age 12

Pleasant Meadows

10 April 2009

Dear Diary

Oh, I am so, so glad to be able to vent out all my feelings, all my excitements to you. I know I ought to be studying right now, but then, I just can't help writing.

Mother, of course, does not understand *everything*! I know she means well – but you know she just can't always help! I just want some rest, some break. And I got such horrid marks in that English test. I was... devastated. But I just couldn't study. And when our teacher was giving the scripts out, she was like," Why Loila, I expected better from *you*. "Like I wasn't feeling bad enough. Honestly, I want to do something worthwhile – I want to be a world famous *author*. And that's why it bothers me about doing badly in *English* so much.

Oh my God! It's seven and I have to study for the Chemistry test. How can I *ever* need Chemistry in my life? I know I need to be more persevering – but I can't; just can't concentrate.

Yours,

Loila

20 April, 2009

Dear Diary,

   I wrote a poem today, and I'm almost sure that it isn't actually bad. My best friend, Rita read it and was like, "Why don't you send it to the papers?"

   I just went, "What?"
   Rita is so sweet. She really supports me. And – guess what, I showed Mom and she went, "Why, it's quite good!"

   I'm going to mail it right away.

   Yours,

   Loila

21 April, 2009

Dear Diary

   I mailed it. The poem, I mean.

   You know today, as I sat in the library, at break, I felt so peaceful, so happy. I felt like it's all a journey. Here I am, striving to realise my dreams; and I'm convinced it's no more than a lovely, pleasurable journey. Of *course* there are the hurdles – but once you get through them, it's lovely. I'm sure – I'm determined that I will get through this journey, and reach the destination.

Hang on! I must add that I managed to scrape through Chemistry. But I am so mad at the boys. Today at Games, I was so busy thinking out my new poem that I totally missed the ball. And they just went, "Can't you even field properly?" And I was like," No I jolly well can't!" Tell me, how am I *ever* going to concentrate in Games - or Algebra - or Science when I'm so busy thinking out my *poems*?"

 Yours,

  Loila

10 May, 2009

Dear Diary,

 Oh, I am so happy... I feel I'm going to burst with happiness! Oh, my poem got published! I'm not even kidding. It's so – o great ... I feel like it's a dream. But then it's a beautiful meadow in the journey, where the traveller gets to rest their weary selves and gather fruit. Course, I don't know what's ahead of me, but this meadow *is heavenly*.

 Yours

  Loila

   (the happiest girl in the world!)

Anirban Datta Gupta
Kolkata, India
Age 14

The Journey of Amun-Den to the New Land

Long ago, in a forgotten age,
Lay a city bright and splendid.
It was fair, and much more;
And its name was Mener-Did.

In it there lived, a sage of old,
And at his last, while dying,
He told his son, the great Amun-Den,
Of what the future was supplying.

"The City ends, for the King is dead,
And his heir is unworthy.
He uses power to whim, and so we will,
Be destroyed unless we be mighty.

So ere he makes you all his slaves,
Flee, with greatest speed.
Leave, and let the fool rule no one,
Leave the great Mener-Did."

And so did Amun-Den, knight of the king
Of before, who ruled so wisely,
Take his men, and kin, and set
Out to leave the country.

They walked through forests and valleys,
Knowing not, to where they went.
Only in the face of mortal danger did they halt
Striding until their strength was spent.

The perilous journey they undertook,
Was riddled with fear and dread,
For thief Kings, and evil things, there were
That never went to bed.

When once attacked by a fearful monster,
Whose dark breath and mane,
Did nearly blind their watchful eyes,
They slew, it and went on again.

At last, wearied in body and mind
They reached there, where ocean and sky did unite.
And on sunrise, spoke Amun-Den "Halt! For in this man-less shore,
The awakening sun marks the rise of our new land, and the end of night."

Ankita Gupta
Kolkata, India
Age 14

A Letter to Whom it May Concern

Hello there, if you are there at all,

No, I did not really hear you call.

You see, I notice everyone praying to you

And sit down to meditate,

They usually look offended if I refuse or hesitate.

But if you are as powerful as everybody claims,

Why do you need to have so many different names?

Sorry, no offence, but isn't that what 'BAD' people do?

Adopt 'Aliases' and 'AKAs", does that apply to you too?

If I say this aloud, I'll be called absurd,

And will also be made sure that little children have not heard.

I have been accompanied by my family

To temples and have seen your idols,

Some look angry, some look old,

Some look serene and saintly,

The majority is made of Gold.

How can all of them be you? I don't understand.

For voicing my thoughts, why am I threatened with

reprimand?

It's not that I disbelieve, I just need some proof,

It's not that I know too much, you're always so aloof.

They say people attain salvation,

But I've never heard your voice,

Just a soft whisper would have done,

I was not expecting noise.

Do I believe? Or do I not?

People kill in your name and I don't quite like it a lot.

Why don't 'You' talk to them? Who's the hypocrite?

It's unfortunate that I don't have the power to choose,

as I see fit.

Freedom of thoughts-my thoughts are my own,

But then I'll be ostracized, I'll be left all alone.

Take a look at what others think- I'm impertinent.

insolent, indolent

If only I knew what they really meant.

I'm just another girl, a non-entity,

I just want to know if you're aware of my identity.

I'm shutting my mind firmly from thinking anymore,

I'll stop with the arguing, it only leaves me feeling sore.

I'll wait till I hear from you, and then I'll decide

Whether by 'You' or by myself, I need to abide.

I'll be waiting for a reply, I need the answer, you see

And now, I'm signing off, Goodbye, Yours truly, ME.

Siddhartha Haldar
Kolkata, India
Age 11

A Journey Through Space

It was a fine Saturday morning and I woke up with the bright glittering rays of sun falling on my eyes. It was my 12th birthday. My parents entered my room singing a birthday carol and gifted me a present wrapped with fine red paper (which is one of my favourite colours) and I was hugged by my parents. I had a bashing birthday. According to my Dad's advice, I had to open the gifts that I received on my birthday. First, I opened my parent's gift and it was neither a book or a toy nor a game CD, but it was a telescope. I was so very happy because it was always my dream to have glance of the space. So the evening after, I sat on my bed and I saw through the telescope, that the moon was shining as white as chalk. I went on an imaginary journey, a journey of the extraordinary brilliance, a journey painted with colours of black, gold, white and yellow, a journey filled with clusters of stars – the journey space was something that no human being (except astronauts) could ever dream of.

I felt that I was really in an actual spacecraft wearing the true white astronaut suit and all equipments fitted to it. I was able to feel the calmness, stillness and quietness of space as I went through the mesmerizing and outstanding journey of space. I had gone deep into space. The clusters of stars were like florists selling garlands of white jasmines in the boutique. There were a few stars placed in a long line which did seem as if white milk was being spilt from the bottle.

I think that this is the reason why scientists call our galaxy the Milky Way'. Each star seemed to be the houses of a countryside area. Then suddenly through the silence of space there came a silvery shooting star with the trails of silver fumes behind it. Space is actually very dark but it is lit up by the bright colours of the stars. I was completely engrossed into this imaginary space journey of mine.

I soon realised that it was quite late and it was time for me to go to bed. I was not quite willing to close off but I couldn't just forget about the journey through space that had been really gifted by God. I had never thought I would experience a space journey. This was a memorable journey through space in my dream.

Raahat Kaduji
Banbury, UK
Age 13

Your Journey is Just Beginning

Opening my eyes for the first time
My first step into a new life
Being cradled in my mother's arms
Not knowing how to read or how to write
With only a scream and a cry to communicate
Unaware of my surroundings
With nothing to worry about
And no difficulties to face
But my journey is just beginning

Old enough to walk and talk
Now in school
Learning, speaking, reading, writing
Earning award stickers whenever I get something right
Being able to converse with my parents
And finally being able to eat on my own
Getting to play whenever I like
And wherever I like
But my journey is just beginning

I'm now classed as a young adult, a teenager
Secondary school has come so fast
Receiving homework everyday
And instead of play I revise and study
Adolescence is hard but fun
And now I can read things and make sense of them
There are some things I still don't understand
And I still can't see why my parents get so stressed
But my journey is just beginning

Whether you're young, old or still don't know
There are some things that you will never get the answer to
Life is challenging but can be enjoyable
The journey is tough but worth it
And whenever you think your time is up
Just think to yourself
That Your Journey is Just Beginning

Kanishk Kanakia
Kolkata, India
Age 12

Blackberry's Journey to the Moon

Blackberry, my pet German Shepherd,
About his journey have you heard?

Well, let me tell you about him first,
He is handsome, friendly and robust.

He is a mischievous pup I must say,
Always hyper and ready to play.

Gosh, he is a naughty guy,
Always stealing biscuits on the sly.

One night, from our terrace he spotted the moon.
And that is when he thought he must have this silver balloon.

He barked and jumped to catch the moon,
He simply went mad as he wanted his balloon.

He was a dog on a mission,
Ready to jump off the ledge without permission.

That's when I realised, what I had to do,
A silver ball I procured in about an hour or two.

He was fascinated by the gleaming object in my hand,
He wanted it instantly and wondered how it looked so grand!

I threw it down, into the garden and it landed with a thud,
Blackberry ran after it, to find his moon in the mud.

He was thrilled and so was I,
After all, he had got his moon.

There shall be peace now, I thought with a sigh,
But, I knew I had spoken too soon.

For now Blackberry had spotted the sun,
Before he embarked on his new journey, I thought I must run!!!!!

Every few days, Blackberry is on a new journey,
Well, that is how he is, my dog - he is so funny!

Nur Kose
Newark, USA
Age 11

Trip to Bangladesh

"Oh no!" my siblings and I exclaimed as we reached a dead-end. In front of us lay a river. We had just been through a 20-hour plane ride to Bangladesh, our mother's native land. Then we had rented a mini-van. We were happy that we only had 20 miles left to reach our mother's village. But we were astonished when the van clattered along the bumpy road for two whole hours. The trip would have taken half an hour in the States. But the window scenes had kept us entertained. Then the road had suddenly disappeared and there was river in front of us.

"What'll we do?" my sister groaned.

My brother Yusuf waved his arms, shouting to the people on the other side of the river. But no one could hear him.

"This is really exciting," my brother Furkan said. "It's just like our father told us it would be!" We looked at the water again. Soon, we noticed a small rowboat tied to a tree. An excited look came into Furkan's eyes. "I know!" he exclaimed. "I'll row the boat to the other side and get the people there to come and pick you up with the ferry."

"That's a great idea!" I exclaimed.

That night, as we climbed into bed, we were all excited to experience some of the stories that our parents had fascinated us with. We realised that this was just the beginning of many adventures that we would encounter in Bangladesh!

Rajashree Mahanty
Kolkata, India
Age 12

A Different Journey

Rita, a twelve-year old girl, was obsessed by the pictures of sea beaches, mountains and historical monuments. But her family being a poor one could not afford travelling.

One day, she discovered the key to a very different kind of journey. Sitting on the sofa with eyes closed she imagined a beach. In her mind, slowly but steadily a vision appeared. Vast stretches of sand with tall mountains with peaks appear to have touched the sky on one side and blue-green waves of the sea lapping against the shore on the other. Through her mind, Rita felt herself amidst the beach. She could actually feel the salty sea air striking her face with a string and as the waves curled around her bare feet, she looked up in awe and wonder at the mountains. The wind whipped her hair around her face and she could feel sand all over her. The sun was setting just then and the sky was splashed with colours of all kinds. Her mind was at an eternal bliss. Somewhere distantly she heard her name being called but she could not bear to tear herself away from the sight of the sea. Suddenly, a tremendous wave came towards the shore. Rita remained rooted to the spot. Her mind screamed with fear and anguish but her feet numb. Then the wave hit the shore. It jerked Rita right off her feet and suddenly everything started spinning and she found herself staring up at her mother, bemused.

Mrittika Majumdar
Kolkata, India
Age 12

My Journey to your Land

"Journeys" is a lovely word for birds like me,
It symbolizes freedom, peace, loneliness, but lots of liberty,
I feel at the top of the world when I think of journeys,
When I think- I'll neglect sadness, crime and poverty.

I am a lonely little swallow,
Travelling over many, many lands,
Crossing valleys, plateaus and seas,
Finally my destination comes at hand.

I start my journey at the eve of autumn,
When it turns a bit chilly,
When the leaves shrivel and fall,
I know it's time for a tour, thus I feel jolly.

Finally I take off,
Not deciding where to go,
But I know, the purpose is,
To escape the harsh winter foe.

I fly on and on,
I see the lushly green,
Some bearing colourful and wild flowers,
Dressing the world like a lissom queen.

Lots of clouds sail along,
The cool breeze blows by,
Airplanes rush along,
And small birds wave me and say "Hi".

I pass the Happy Prince,
I look into his eyes,
I remember how we together helped that family.
I feel he is so noble and wise.

At night, the stars called me,
They asked me if I saw Africa,
I said, "I don't know,
Maybe I did, but is that near India?"

I reach now- I look back at the experience of the traverse,
I remember many a lovely view,
Friend, I'm here in your city,
And I hope to meet you....

Haala Marikar
Matale, Sri Lanka
Age 9

Wonder Full Vehicle

A Journey By Horse Goes By A Trot,
Clippity - Clop, Clippity - Clop!
They Run At A Fast Pace,
As If There Were Some Race.

A Journey By Cart Is Pulled By A Bull,
So Mind Not To Make The Cart Too Full.
The Farmer Stays At The Front,
In Case The Bull Becomes Too Blunt

A Journey By Van,
We Need A Water Can,
For Going On A Far Journey
We'll Become Thirsty.

A Journey By Bike,
We Don't Have To Hike,
But We Have To Make Sure That Both
The Wheels
Has It's Daily Petrol Meals.

A Journey By Car,
We Can Go Far,
And It's Steering Wheels
It's Made Of Steel.

But Walking Alone
We Can Do It On Our Own
For We Don't Have To Drive Our Own Legs
It Gives Us A Feeling Good And Steady
And Then When We Want To Go Somewhere
We'll Always Be Ready

Sarah Murphy
Cheltenham, UK
Age: 14

A Thousand Wing Beats Away

Like cormorants topped with lazy straw hats,
Fishermen balance on the rocks, their faces
tanned as slabs of agate mud, staring out
to the watercolour shadow of a peak –

the jade-adorned empress reigning over
an angry violet swell, frothing at the mouth,
foam waves lacing the fishermen's feet
like the pearls whispering in their corrugated prisons
at the bottom of a sun-baked sea.

Shadowing the forest –
a canopy of spider webs, morning dew
glistening on gossamer threads, the scarlet and
black legs of the eight-eyed tenants scuttling:
reckless acrobats on a skeletal tightrope.

Lolling banana leaves rustle overhead,
chattering softly in yellow tones, beside the
silent towers of bamboo, watching quietly
with fluted eyes.

A charcoal-eared kite flaps proudly above,
darting behind golden tinged clouds
at the sight of a metal bird, its wings taut and severe,
clawing sad rents through the untouched blue.

A thousand wing-beats away,
raindrops make wet footprints down a pane,
paled fingers tracing their journey.

Hollow-eyed pigeons stalk the grass of cement,
with legs like cocktail sticks and squawks for songs.
Greedy beaks snatch tasteless crumbs and steal away,
Their papery wings mocking.

The mountains are steel giants
soulless spires piercing the blemished sky,
tears rolling openly from its gaping grey eyes.

But then a chink of light gleams through,
a brass-gold drop tinting the edge of a memory:
A frail cobweb lies across the window, a silver loom;
there's the patter of dove-blue feet, shakily moving
along the thread,

to the other side.

Aindrila Pal
Kolkata, India
Age 13

The Sailing Spirit of Journeys

Journeys are like the mind of a poet, covering unknown distances to unfurl the mystical secrets of nature. As we let our minds and souls cross barriers, splash through gurgling streams, walk through fresh, green meadows, white sheets of snow, we realise that journeys are not merely large distances covered geographically as all passé travel-books would say. In fact it is an eternal recreation of our minds and bodies, in finding our true selves and devoting time to our weary spirits.

Journeys are so like the flame of a candle, sometimes flickering to grow dim, sometimes ablaze, symbolising the ups and downs of journeys, where you can never see the future unlike the horizon of the sea against a setting sun. Assuming dancing shapes, the burning of a candle is a journey itself-symbolic of the journey of life. Journeys are so varied, like a cloisonné, where the more colour and polish you add, the more strength and vibrancy is brought about. Journeys by bus, car, and train, what brings life into them are time, patience and optimism. So if you are on a bicycle journey, release all your worries, let your freedom grow wings, steer your bicycle through the roughest of roads and you will soon feel the adrenaline rush and your heartbeats crying out in happiness. And as somebody had famously said, money cannot buy everything including the true spirit of journeys. All you need is the sailing spirit of optimism to brighten up journeys.

Priyanjana Pramanik
Kolkata, India
Age 15

All the Difference

I picked up a flower today
It was the most perfect blossom I had ever seen
And I stopped on my way back home
Dazzled, for a minute, by the tiny glimmer of light
Startling on a dull, cloudy day.

Would you be surprised to hear me say
I risked my life for that tiny bloom?
I did not see the car that came
Or the men who ogled as I bent over
I picked it up
And someone snickered, I did not hear
 I wondered how I could be given joy
By something that they could not see.

I do not know, I do not presume to know
Why my journey is as no one else's
And yet, if all journeys began at a point
Whence each one diverged-
It is odd to think that they shall meet
No matter how diverse,
And all joys and sorrows will be one.

When my few days have come and gone
I may not say that I have won
And yet… I'll know I have not lost
My last days will not go too fast,
Full of regrets as so many are
I have faith at least that far…
I refuse to live my life like those
Who live and breathe only in name
My path and theirs will never meet
No more and no less can I claim.

Anuradha Rao
Chennai, India
Age 15

A Journey of Friendship

Years ago, I'd never thought
Our camaraderie
Would be a most memorable,
Cherished odyssey.

Though I had a flaring temper
Which no one else could stand-
She accepted me for who I was,
We set off hand in hand....

She always made me feel wanted
Never failed to show she cared
Happiness, mirth, pleasure
And merriment we shared.

We had many petty squabbles
But compromise followed strife
Our journey- the piece that completed
The jigsaw of my life.

But she was led astray, and I
Felt an inexplicable dearth
Sleepless nights, sorrowful tears
Helped me see her true worth.

Reunion saw intimacy grow
And the birth of selfless love
Without her, I would be like
A single mismatched glove.

She redefined the word 'friend'
I enjoyed her company
I confided, sought advice
With her, I'd just be me!

I had many pals, but somehow
She stood out from the rest
I don't know what I meant to her
To me, she was the best!

We became close companions
Inseparables- side by side,
I didn't envy her talent and chic
Her achievement was my pride!

We'd long traversed the same route
But we each had dreams to chase
My heart broke as the road forked
For it was time to part ways.

Now at the brink of separation
Memories engulf my mind
May our paths repeatedly cross,
I look longingly behind....

Our journey together ends here
We'll soon be far apart
But she'll always occupy
A special place in my heart.

Amitrajit Sarkar
Kolkata, India
Age 15

Sands of Time

Siddhartha was never much for journeys. Destinations suited him just fine. Brought up in the extravagant safety of his palace, he had seldom seen beyond the high walls of his castle, except for an occasional hunting expedition or two, and even less so stepped out of the confines of his cosy carriage. His parents merely wished him to be happy. So they delivered him from the harsh frailties of the world, to a place where little could touch him – neither pain, nor, as it happened, pleasure. He passed from one day to the other, from one muse to another, entertained and yet not so. Sometimes when one has too much and there is naught wanting, one needs a little nothing. So deep into the night one day he decided to take a walk, not just through the resolute arched hallways of his palace, but through the desolate walkways of his kingdom. He told nobody, he took none with him, but stole away in silence in the middle of the night. The moon shone bright through the starry night and streamed through the royal gardens. The only one who saw the prince leave was the kingly swan in her bed of light.

The ways were dusty and the path hard. His shoes grew dirty and his legs felt sore. He trudged along with woeful tread, with the firm resolve to let loose something out of his system, but what he knew not. He cherished the solitude of his newfound independence, but felt strangely vacant and empty inside without his usual array of courtiers and jesters tailing him. Was there no one to walk beside him? Was this journey his to make alone? Well, there was a man beneath the boughs of the tree. Perhaps he would offer pleasant company. Walking up to the man he realised, to his horror, that he was mistaken. The gnarly old figure, fatigued by fever was writhing in pain in the shadows of the Pipal. Siddhartha retracted, aghast. The emperor's son stumbled and fell to his knees. He couldn't bear to look, but he saw a man walk up from behind him into the dark grasp of the tree with a glass of water, which he calmly fed the man's parched throat before returning to the light. With shrunken shoulders the boy asked the man, "Will he be alright?" The serene eyes whispered back, "He can only feel a little better."

"Where have you been?" asked the anxious Queen. The Prince had returned, and stood with his back to the closed doors, the moon on his broad shoulders and crown. "Just out for a walk, and no more," returned the Prince. And yet he was a Prince no more. He was a King.

Yu Ching Tan
Singapore
Age 15

The Travelling Fire

ignited; the fire burns
he has long outstretched fingers in the shape of flames
everything he touches, he destroys.
down the road, a little valley
down the valley, a little village
down the village, a little home

in the home, there lives a little family
in the family, there lives a little cat
in the cat, he smells something
in the cat, his pulse quickens

speeding aside his heartbeat, the little cat hears his
instincts
he warns them of the danger
the dance of the fire is getting warmer and
a little too close for comfort.

the fire does not think.
the fire does not wait.
down the road he strolls.
down the valley he saunters
down the village he treads

goodbye home,
goodbye family,
goodbye cat.
you tried your best.

but after the fire has done what he needs to do;
after he has ruined everything in his path
there is but one thing left to do:

he will turn back on himself

Rida Vaquas
Mile Oak, Staffs, UK
Age 12

Roots

Watch the bird nest in that tree,

*The birds have always been beautiful,
In both Pakistan and Britain,
Though in different ways,
Still beautiful.*

Do you know how it is possible?
For a tree to be able to hold on to so much life;
It is because it has healthy roots-
Strong roots,
Firm roots.

*And so do my family,
Roots that always lead us back;
To Pakistan.
No matter how fluent our English is,
No matter that both me and my brother were both born in England,
Our origin, our roots lay deep underground in Pakistani soil.*

A tree is nothing without its roots,
No matter how tall it is,
It may be one of the mighty trees of the Amazon;
But if the roots are damaged or cut off,
The tree will simply die;
And no matter how much grandeur it sustained in its lifetime;
It will simply become an ugly rotting thing,
The decadence almost painful to look at.

Alas for trees it is easy to damage their roots,
What are they?
Just a physical thing,
It is easy to damage a physical thing is it not?
But familial bonds, the memories of childhood for my parents,
The remembrance of food, the Pakistani TV channels you get on SKY,
The sorrow they feel,
When their beloved country appears on the news;
It's hard to break away from it all.
And I'm glad they didn't;
Thanks to them;
I'm a British-Pakistani:
A bird migrating between cultures,
And proud.

The News

Flickering grotesque images,
On the television screen,
So far away, disconnected from me.
Another bomb blast,
A small flinch.

Vaguely wonder why;
No injuries on me.
Of course wasn't there,
Wasn't there to behold;
Degradation of my beloved homeland,
Chaos raging throughout,
Doubt why.

Mind wanders back,
To eating chaat on vacation
To collection of salwaar kameez;
Journey back to sounds, smells, sights, touches, tastes;
Relatives, alive or dead?
Riding on speculative train of thought.

Self conditioned to be British,
But have a somewhat Pakistani heart:
Which broke at the news today.

Politics, politics, politics
I don't care,
All I know,
People of my country are dying,
Innocents.

And I'm just watching the news,
Just letting it happen,
Just watching it as if it was a show;
Silent vow to save them,
Not sure how.

Fires, people jobless,
People not knowing whether their son will come home;
So many people dead,
Without the chance to say 'I love you' to those important.
Cruel, bloody slaughter,
Performed by heartless monsters.

Soundlessly wonder if it could've been me,
My life torn apart,
My parents gone.

The city I treasure in my heart;
Karachi.

And people will go on about their lives,
For no one can afford to stop;
Every life taken, ruined, destroyed, torn apart,
The ones in charge will never know,
The extent of damage done.
I do,
And I will journey back to Karachi;
Save the souls left behind,
Rebuild it back to the city,
In cherished memories.

Chua Jun Yan,
Singapore
Age 14

A Propeller's Coo

Before the 'unrooted' label took root

I stumbled on a bumboat ride along Collar Quay
In a frenzied jig I danced aboard
With seconds to go before the whistle blew
The propellers cooed on the beat, hurtling us forward like a lullaby

Along the bank, I strained my brain
To picture the shop houses and coolies from History class
But a whitewash of cafes (al fresco, at that) deluged my mind
As foreign tongues wagged against the waves
The propellers cooed on the beat, hurtling us forward like a lullaby

Downstream, where postcard depicts,
A bustling port with global links
The only sign of trade I saw, was concealed
Beneath the facade of skyscrapers over the CBD
The propellers cooed on the beat, hurtling us forward like a lullaby

At the mouth, I sniffed a lungful of our colonial past
Here where neo-classical architectural reigned
In a cocktail of irony and Asian pride
The flag of a young nation fluttered outside Parliament House
Still the propellers cooed on the beat, hurtling us forward like a lullaby

I set off to explore a forgotten past
Through the dual lenses of space and time
But ashore, all that left of my journey,
Was a ticket stub in hand.
Then, the propellers shut off

Writers aged 16 and over

Sabrina Ahmad
Dhaka, Bangladesh

Rewind

January had sunk her freezing teeth into this sleepy Manikganj village, and everyone else had taken advantage of the *kombol* weather by bundling into their blankets as soon as it was dark. Pushing my balled fists deeper into the pockets of my sweatshirt, I surveyed the dirt track that led me down my solitary midnight walks whenever I visited the NGO. The moon was a ghostly glow piercing the fog of the night, dyeing everything with a silvery sheen without really illuminating anything, but I knew memory would guide my feet better than my eyesight could.

We had met on this very road three years ago.

"All I want is someone who will listen to me" you had told me, on the third night that you joined me on my walk.

I grew quiet, letting you speak. The cold air, the wet, earthy smell of the cauliflower patch, and your stories accompanied me back to Dhaka.

I found you again on this road the next year. Our fingers locked on the third trip around the circuit, and I held my breath when you began to speak.

"I don't think this is going to work out."

The breeze makes waves over the moonlit lake, creating fairy sparkles as I draw to the end of my first lap around the circuit. As I approach the quarters, I find a familiar figure standing there. *This cannot be real.*

You look away, biting your lips, unable to meet my eyes.

"Mind if I join you?"

Sairah Akhtar
Smethwick, UK

Lost and Found

The road is no longer visible; the trees, the houses, the river, they're all gone. Walking up the dusty pathway, my mind travels back seven years, when my life turned upside down. The sounds of guns echo in my head. The smell of blood, stings my nose, evoking memories best forgotten. I remember the heart-rending, heart-breaking pain I felt, standing still amongst the anarchic chaos, looking at a boy of about five, with mud, tears and blood covering half of his face and body. He was as quiet as a thief cloaked with the darkness of the night, with tears streaming down his face. The excruciating pain I felt for this lost boy was akin to the pain I felt with a broken arm, broken leg, dislocated shoulder and bruised ribs. The relief I felt when I was brought to this new land overwhelmed me. It gave me the chance to escape to somewhere where security and safety were guaranteed. Rubbing my eyes, I mentally shake my head free of plaguing memories. This is my home. The journey I took to escape brought me back here for a reason. There are no remnants of the massacre, but it's still there; intertwined with the foundations of the land. My journey was one of heart and soul; to find acceptance, something that wasn't found in a foreign land. Returning home signals the end of my journey and maybe with time acceptance will come too.

Mir Mahfuz Ali
Kingston-upon-Thames, UK

When Bangladesh Floats in a Water-hyacinth

I will visit you in silence
when my country floats
in a water-hyacinth,
and ponder how much
I know of your flavour
by catching boaal
and chital fish together.
I will walk the sunset
that loses itself
in your plum-black water.
I have come to admire
the resilience of this tiger land
where the snake takes on a life
quicker than my hands,
adding its signature
branch by branch,
then surprises me
when the floodwater returns
over and over to take up
the same monsoon swirls.
Rice grasses rustle
as I row my pleasure boat over
their smallest leaning
and it is time, once again
to get to know
the clay at the river-bottom
that colours my skin
like comforting chocolate.

Bangladesh Began in Rain

Ah my beguiling Bangladesh! Did you really begin your life
in rain? I am a thirst.

I want to drink the slogans of rye grass
and sing the poison of rattan-berry thorns.

My name is ingrained in your rice-step rivers
flowing from the black thighs of Himalayas.

Plunge me in your music. I am a fine composer. The tunes I
will hum
will become bulbul notes that only girls can hear. I wait
along the stream for that one girl scooping ripe dung in the
meadow
and slopping it in her wicker basket.

Who could complain about that odour? My sadness for her
is a tide that comes in
twice nightly, as she slaps
a glistening pat on my skin like pita bread on a clay oven.

I am not a Stranger to this World

I am not a stranger to this world.
Ask the bimal bamboo bush
that carries my name
in its long slender canes.
They will tell you I belong
here amongst the jaruls and jamruls
by the clay-pond banks
at the back of the house
where I was born many harvests ago.

I am not a stranger
to the boatman, Kadam Ali,
or the village poet, Folo Bibi
and her roaming ally, Bawool Srimathi.
They might have told you
how I pierced the pitchers
on girls' head with my sling shots,
soaking their kortas and kamizes.
But you should have heard
how I played naked
in the monsoon mud
with Saima Nanda.

I am not a stranger
to the smell of the earth.
Many times I helped Jabor Ullah
plough the hard land
softened by morning mist.
I saw how he sniffed the odour
of the earth huddled between his arms,
pushed me to understand
the thick richness of cow dung
transforming the field with its slow rot.

I am not a stranger
to the whisper of the alder wood
where decay changed to growth.
Girls on the way to school
walk on the dew of my name.
If you look around
you will find my presence
still holds true inside them,
if you care to lift the past back
to reveal what I have done
before I began a runaway life.

I am not a stranger
to the berries in the bush,
thatching a roof
or building up a hay-sack.
My umbilical cord buried
under that orange tree in June.

Nobody Told Me

Someone could have told me
you have to rot before you ripen.
The days of open fields
and running free, of ruining your shirt
by going into the sugar-canes
with the Hindu girl Nandita,
showing her the language of the bush
in the mist flavoured twilight.
The lilt of her sari roused
the leaves we needed for our art.
A hot tincture in her blouse
drove me wild to be with her mouth.
At first, she turned me away
then she washed me
in that blue rustling bush
while the country glide
inside Nandita's shitala quilt.
Many times we hid under the little candle
of the iced moon, senses tingling
to the last drop of dawn.

Kavita Amarnani
Brighton, UK

My Grandmother's Laugh

My Grandmother is no longer alive. But I can see her now, with papery, olive skins and a silver plait.

When we lived in India, my sister and I shared the bed next to her. She used to laugh a lot, which seems strange given her grief-scarred life – disability, disenfranchisement, death after death.

Perhaps there was nothing to lose.

She had a big, silent laugh. Joyous and toothless, it shook her like a jelly.

My sisters and I were playing on the bed next to her the first time we experienced a power cut. Plunged inexplicably into darkness, we thought the world had ended. We opened our mouths and screamed.

My grandmother tried to shout over us, to tell us to be quiet. But she just couldn't stop laughing.

Once I tried to teach her English. Trotting importantly up to her bed, I pointed theatrically to my dress. 'Frock,' I announced.

'Frog,' she replied smiling.

'Frock!' I insisted doggedly.

'Frog,' she persevered.

My growing exasperation tickled her no end. She showed her gums and began to shake.

The day we decided to build a ship out of pillows, they'd just been encased in pristine, freshly laundered pillowcases. We hurled them onto the floor and jumped aboard. My grandmother couldn't believe it. She scolded and appeased and tried to summon up anger as we went about our business. Once or twice we looked at her then carried on. Eventually she gave up, closed her eyes and started laughing.

And laughing.

Asim Anwer Ansari
Uttar Pradesh, India

I Journey

Ever if I could
Stop these rims moving
Over the cracks on road
Through the woods
Near the farms

Ever if I could
Catch these birds flying
Over the clouds
Over the woods
Near the farms

But 1 couldn't
I journey
I move

I'm life.

Ranjit Singh Bahia
Walsall, UK

The Beginning

I walked off the plane and the hot Indian breeze hit my face like a snowball would have hit me in cold England. The smell was unusual like the smell of the woven bags that rice would have come out. Before I had reached the bottom of the steps of the plane my face was already sweating, like it had been water melting from the snowball.
The journey had begun.
The journey through the airport and to the waiting airport population of relations, porters, beggars, sellers police and finally all the anticipating faces of relatives and friends waving for attention was so much to see in such a short time, my eyes tired, my ears ringing, I switched my brain to pause and watched and heard like it was all a silent movie in black and white.
The pause button was released the moment a cockerel made its awakening call, and the sweet sound of Kirtan awoke my inner mind and heart, I had arrived.
The village of my father and ancestors in Northern India Punjab, was called Kukar Pind, it was here that my journey of discovery and belonging had begun.

The sweet smell of village life, the small alleys, the place where my father was born and where he remained in his youth until he left for England, all made my body and mind feel at ease as I now knew where the journey had begun, and as I lay outside looking at the stars on my munja (straw bed) I knew that I was in the right place to discover how I was born in England, who I was, and where I had come from. My journey was just at the beginning.

Amrita Bandopadhyay
Kolkata, India

Home Tonight

The blinding white light and walls hurt Indu as she tried to focus. It was an abrupt awakening from a terrifyingly intense dream: a dream so vivid that her surroundings seemed unreal. She might still be dreaming. What if she rushed out of the apartment and found herself on the lane extending from the house of the Dasguptas to that of the Kidwais? She would run out on the wide road where the men and women would sit with their food, vegetables and fish. One solitary mad woman would scream filth at the heavens. She would stare at the ceaseless traffic; then walk back home, her head high in the air, aware of the glances shot by sympathetic and curious neighbours. She would wonder whether she should have caught a bus and brought her father back as his moronic mistress would stare in her magenta nightgown. Indu is sixteen once more.

She smiled, recalling Pratap's concerned face as he examined her with clinical precision. Indu dragged her frail, inert limbs out of the bed and stood by the window. The city of New York gleamed, throbbing incessantly. Higher up, she looked at the moon: her namesake. It was unusually big and luminous. It was a festive night in Calcutta. Her grandmother would have everything in order: the rituals, the best food and sweets. Moments stood in elixir-like perfection. Indu folded her hands and imagined the wise benign goddess in white. A tear stained her cheek as a prayer uttered itself.

Juhi Basoya
New Delhi, India

She Travels

She travels
Far and wide
Seeking
Healing
Fulfilment
A connection
Forever moving
Even when still
Sometimes mesmerized
Sometimes repulsed
Until
A journey within
Growing
Learning
Discovering
The vast, infinite
Me
Peace

Compass Travels

I traverse the blank slate that could have been the sky had it not been for its colour. I am far away from home. From where I stand, home is a small dot in the centre of a vast open space. I look at it with amazed fondness as I realize that home is always my final resting place. I may fly across the universe, span continents, jump oceans, but home is where I always return. Each time I expand the circle of my comfort to explore new dimensions, each time I return. To rest and to find new beginnings; like the leaves return to earth, the sea to the clouds and man to dust. This is the circle of life. Just like the charcoal circle I create as I traverse space. The circle that gives meaning to my existence and defines my purpose. The purpose of a compass in a geometry box.

Michael Brett
London, UK

Bangladesh, London

Everyone thinks they want to go home.
Like tube trains unwinding, Himalayan rain
Runs in streams through the trees of Nepal
And everyone wants to go home.

In shops, queues that make you think of the Ganges
Uncoiling like a snake across the delta,
Past trees that wave goodbye like hands,
Everyone thinks of home. They think

It will all be the same as when they left:
When planes bounce onto runways,
When Hajiis in white return from Mecca,
As waterborne Hindu ashes yearn
In clouds towards the bay.

When you dream of home,
You dream of a green horizon like a green smile,
Of home tucked beneath plump and nurturing clouds
Like sheep, and familiar streets, shops and smells.

But they are gone.
They are lost beneath a cyclone of road signs, blocks
And tenements.

Your home only exists here in London,
In a Ganges of the mind,
Beneath its waters and bent by time,
Where waves beat like closing doors
And mud in the water is a drawn down blind.

Everyone wants to go home, but this is home.

London-from Aqaba to Zem Zem

Once all we wanted was a little space:

When the kitchen and the cooking pots did not seem big enough,
When-at home-even the President's giant rooms were crazed
With marauding soldiers stripping bath taps, lights and mirrors.
Then nothing could seem big enough.
When men are dangerous, space is safety.

Then the largest spaces, ocean or desert,

Have a voiceless call and motion.
Then sandy ribs of dunes are waves
And Atlantic waves are dunes and
Inside their pulse, the longing for a space

Unbracketed by time or maps becomes unendurable.
Then the London A to Z stands for London
From Aqaba to Zem Zem.
This London runs through people like the Silk Road.
Its end is no mysterious gunshot or sari drenched in petrol.

Here the wider world is not a cheap and crackling radio, but
Like a distant star both real and dreamlike. It is something far away,
Dull and like a number on a celestial map,
But as close and brilliant as the brightest jewel in the ear
Of the darkest passenger next to you on the tube.

Beneath an aircraft wing, London twists like the crowd
That spins around the Kaaba. Delirious as a fishing reel,
It spools you in. In a café in a London street
I hear my native language. Let me translate for you,
They are worried about the tax man not the secret police.

Arun Budhathoki
Kathmandu, Nepal

A Farewell Note

Now that I'll be
Gone

This place is busy erasing me--
within, without

the objects that I belonged to--
movin' out and rest will wither away soon

It keeps me in people's memory
That I know
Soon they will forget me too
Because memory isn't permanent

Perhaps a photo will do or a note
But they too will rot away soon

mine touch, fingerprints, Myself--
Replaced

Now that I'll be
Gone

This place is busy missing me--
within, without

I will miss it too--
its heat, polluted air and ruined metropolis

Now that I'll be
Gone

This place is busy forgetting me--
within, without

It's a century old tradition
You come and go
You occupy and abandon
You're remembered and forgotten

Now that I'll be
Gone

I'm busy erasing, missing and
forgetting this place

I've no other choice--
I'm decaying

A Train Journey

Ahesta boro, my sluggard train, ahesta boro.

Under the vehement sun
these prison-like cells
reels as the endangered
Earthworm

nibbling the delirious soil

In this cave
insanity is a cheap product
you buy and sell

In this dungeon
cynicism is a cheap food
you consume and digest

these eyes—
drugged

It's senseless, lifeless

Only dreams to be with loved ones

Ahesta boro, my sluggard train, ahesta boro.

Confession

This is the city that terrifies me most
The sky is punched black-blue
I hide within warm walls
And act like a dying mosquito

The street is the metallic palm
Reading its lines
The future is dark, dark

Not oxygen
I smell parasites in the air
Every face I see
It's the forbidden cave

And darker that I am
This the heart that terrifies me most

Safia Chaudhary
Hounslow, UK

Before

This is how it should be,
The sun glinting off the minarets
Lapis lazuli, blue like the ocean
On the calmest of days.
The crystal sand and the dusty roads
Yellow grains of beautiful earth
Crunch under sandaled feet.
Mosaic tiling on the walls of the schools
Whirling patterns of endless colour
Smooth and cold under your fingertips.

This is how it should be,
The hustle and bustle of the covered bazaar
Incense and heavy spice and the fresh scent of pine needles
Assail your senses
Tantalisingly close and drawing you in.
Oranges, sweet and ripe
Sticky juice dripping down your hands and around your mouth
Refreshing in the desert heat
You would not swap for any other life.

This is how it should be
Women with their coloured chadors draped around their heads
Manoeuvring the crowds in their haste to get home
Men amble along the road, sandals dragging in the dust
Stop to talk to a friend of a friend by the roadside
Ask how the family is doing.
Children laugh and play in the alleys and courtyards
Their footsteps and smiles echoing off the marble and cloth
That holds up the sky,
Grandparents chide them for their speed,
Lost in the slow ascent of old age.

This is how it used to be,
Before

Life and Myself

I've been on a journey since I met you
Somewhere, once upon a time
I've travelled all the well worn paths
And counted all the miles
I've grown up since I met you
Become more than what I was
I've learnt my lessons the hard way
And found peace in the two of us
I've been where angels fear to tread
And come out with head held high
I've lost enough to know what's safe
And moulded a whole new life.
I've been on a journey since I found you
Within this heart of mine
It's good to know I know me
I'm the peace I find inside.

Pervin Chhapkhanawala
Pune, India

What's in a Name?

Sandhya darted towards the lobby of ThreeSpeak and flashed her identity card at a black instrument on the door. It instantly parted and she was swallowed by the huge steel and glass structure. Sandhya checked her watch – 2:25 p.m. She had only five minutes to reach the eighth floor, walk through a maze of cubicles and receive her first call.

Stepping in the lift, looked into the mirror, rolled behind her shoulders and set her hair in place. The manual had contained everything she needed from accent stressors, response sheets, diagrams and sketches, to a summary of make-up and hairstyle hints. These large BPOs would stop at nothing. Just Rakesh to Rocky or Kavita to Kate was not good enough; they etched out an entire personality makeover.

"Yes, the weather is awful today!" Sandhya blurted into the mirror. She mentally put a tick against her accent. The right amount of swallowing of letters, the correct speed. *'They can hear your smile over the miles'* she remembered. Who would believe that a shy, confused girl lay beneath that bubbly voice? Moody, dishevelled, Sandhya who loved Pav Bhaji, hated the sight of ambulances in traffic and lived with eight other people in a two bedroom flat.

The lift stopped and she manoeuvred her way through the maze to a cubicle. She sat down, sighed, shut her eyes and pasted a smile on her lips. She clicked. "Good morning! This is Sandra. How may I help you?"

Kshama Chhapkhanawalla
Mumbai, India

Musical Chairs

I start from the oceans to merge back in one,
A journey of a million intertwined lifetimes
I have been the tree, the moonlight, the sun,
The soil beneath my soul and the wind in the chimes.

I transgress, I progress, I move alone with crowds
After one life breathes the next, like a pendulum's to and fro
Rings of hopes lost, loves ignored and silent seeking shouts
Each journey is a wink but their visions drift slow.

I am jolted by my purpose, to dig out the eventual truth
My karma forms the links of a necklace hanging loose
But my strength's waning now; I no longer hear the flute
I need to fly free before the necklace becomes the noose.

Kashif Choudhry
Solihull, UK

The Patriarch

The lines on your hands

Led to lands left far behind

A mountainous grave

An unfulfilled wish remained

Your prayer upon our lips.

Sala Choudhury
Southampton, UK

Same to Same

Ahmed scanned the street. The roads were filled with litter, a beggar sat in a door frame pleading to passersby to donate spare change. Women in burkhas shuffled past hurriedly whilst men spilled on to the street from the mosque. The air was filled with the smell of fresh jalebi and the sound of the latest Bengali folk tune rung in his ears. Ahmed's thoughts were interrupted as a man barged past him; the man turned to look at Ahmed gave an apologetic look before spitting his beetle juice against a wall.
It had taken Ahmed 6 years to save the money for this trip. He had sold all his land and cashed in his savings for this trip of a lifetime. He had travelled 8 hours from his home to the High Commission to apply for a visa. Later he travelled 5 hours to the airport from his village before taking an 11 hour plane half way across the world. In those 6 years he could never have imagined that the streets of London would resemble Bangladesh so much. As his wife would say, it was very same to same.

Renita D'Silva
Chessington, UK

Dreams of Home

On cold overcast London November days, I dream of home...

I am walking barefoot through fields baking in the sun, the mud cracked, dry. The air is heavy, humid. Waiting. I hurry home, skipping nimbly along the path. There's fish curry and red rice awaiting me, and perhaps raw mango chutney. The sun, a yellow ball of fury beats down relentlessly. A light breeze whistles through coconut fronds and gently caresses my perspiration beaded face. Thunder rumbles in the distance and I quicken my step desperate to get home before the heavens open.
The long awaited rain comes just as I finish lunch. I sit on the veranda with a tumbler of tea listening to rain drumming frenziedly on the roof tiles, watching rivulets of water gush out of drains. Coconut trees sway in the breeze and paddy fields transform into pools as the parched soil greedily soaks up rain water. In the far field, women hum a haunting melody as they sow rice saplings, the woven umbrella shelters they wear on their bent backs making them look like giant brown question marks. Their song celebrates the monsoons. They thank the Goddess for saving them from drought again this year.

I awake from my reverie in another country, in a grey, wintery world. I have journeyed thousands of miles away, to London, where my future awaits. But my heart is still nestled among windswept coconut trees and muddy fields; it still thinks of a hot sun-baked country as home...

Salil Desai
Pune, India

For Old Times' Sake

"We lived here," my friend said emotionally.

His son fidgeted. His daughter shuffled awkwardly. No corresponding sentiment lit their eyes, not even curiosity. Just polite boredom!

Sanjay had persuaded me to come along for old times' sake. It was his journey to his roots, after many years abroad. I had been reluctant to make it mine. I hadn't left India.

It wasn't some old, ancestral house – just a typical middle-class apartment.

The children gazed indifferently.

"Remember, we would study here?" Sanjay prodded me, pointing to a corner of the enclosed balcony. The wooden partition of Sanjay's erstwhile personal space was missing, probably removed once his parents shifted to a bigger house and began renting this place out.

"Yes!"

I had been a fool to accompany him.

"We also read umpteen James Hadley Chase paperbacks……!" he reminisced, winking.

Forbidden lurid covers showing busty, voluptuous blondes flashed back at me.

"You also smuggled 'Playboy' once," I replied unguardedly.

He glanced uneasily at the children. Satisfied they were out of earshot, he smiled, "I was terrified my sister Alka might find it while snooping around."

I fought back the nostalgia. It had been a mistake to join Sanjay's journey. Inevitably it had become mine too.

"I kissed Alka in here …..twice," I blurted unexpectedly.

Stunned, he shot a horrified glance at the children.

"Sorry. Didn't mean to shock you! Nothing else happened……"

I knew I had ruined his trip. But at least his children goggled excitedly for the first time. They had heard.

Hartman de Souza
Goa, India

(Untitled)

Last year, had you climbed this hill, behind the same government school and everyday village life, barely two kilometres as a bird would fly, you would have seen first-hand how a thickly forested hill had literally disappeared, leaving in its wake, a huge pit with daunting cliffs dropping to dirty, muddied water at the base. Were you lucky enough to have tried to climb this hill three years before that, its sudden absence would have held you by the throat? It was so thick with tree cover and undergrowth you wouldn't have made it even a quarter of the way up, unless you managed to find one of the paths that villagers here traditionally use. The trees and mud disappeared, the water was sprung and set free to be dirtied with mining waste and eventually die. The hare and porcupines, the wild cats, the wild pig, the leopards and bison all turned refugees.

Today as you drive past the school it is better not to look that way.

Two barren dumps of dirty brown waste towering above specifications form a skyline that children in the school must perforce grow up with as their leaders fatten their already-wide bellies. As if a cry from Mother Earth herself, one solitary tree, far more gigantic than those that fell around it, stands dead and leafless on the slopes of this gigantic pit with its sheer walls and torpid water, like a surreal memorial to one that did not fall to the bulldozers.

Tamsin Evans
Exeter, UK

Six O'clock Meeting

The temple water tank was clogged with lilies, crowded together like teacups and saucers in a sink. I walked along the edge, concentrating on the way the slabs of stone tessellated neatly beneath my feet, trying to stop my heart from racing on ahead. My nerves flipped messy somersaults in my stomach, like a fish out of water. It was the same feeling I used to get before clarinet exams; that quiet, bubbling panic.

The sun was sinking low now and jaundicing the sky and the air was closing in around me with dusk and the scent of the wilting jasmine in my hair.

It was two minutes to six. In two minutes he would be there, at the front of the temple. I wondered if I would recognise him, if I would be able to spot him in the throngs of temple-goers and beggars crowding the steps. I wondered if he would recognise me. All day I'd searched for familiar features in the faces of the middle-aged men I'd passed on the street. Mum said I had his eyes.

Aftab Khan Farooqui
Goa, India

To Mehr 01 - The South of France

Your little milk bottle in my right trouser pocket, you sitting on my lap trying your best to get your own toes into your own mouth, we sat at an Ille sur Tet local bus stop whilst your mother was at driving school across the street. I was trying to whisper good advice into your tiny ears while I watched the French go by. I wanted you to choose carefully in this world. See, some buy fresh bread, some don't, some get into a bus while others drive past in a big car. Some wait, while the smarter ones make others wait. At eleven months and a few odd days, you didn't exactly understand what I was trying to tell you. Every once in a while, you would look up at me to make sure it was your father who was holding her. Sometimes you would yell a little as if to let me know that you were hungry and that it was time for me to pull out that bottle of milk.
Choose well my dear. You are everything to me.
When the world defeats you, don't fall, but catch your breath, assess the situation and then plan your next move. Would you like to take this bus or walk or just sit and watch them all some more my baby?

Love

Papa

Notes to Mehr 04:
The West End, London

London is one of the best cities in today's 2010 GMT world, buzzing with a non-stop rush of Red Bullish adrenalin that oozes out of a rather dysfunctional ball of rhythmic fire. So easy to fall in love here, every weekend that too! Easy to forget long drawn out episodes.
ATM machines called 'Hole In The Wall', true horrors of Jack the Mr. Rippers at Whitechapel Halal shops, contraceptives through vending machines and a fetish to get trashed in each other's faces in a midnight weekend tube train compartment. Relationships are made this way with an undiluted passion for anything in motion in the streets. Everyone seems tightly squeezed. There's constant noise. It's humane and at the same time quite urbane. A supportive mechanism of all things in the action genre. You may wonder if the bodies in the graveyard listen to the tubes and dance to its chaos. People can't even sit still in photos!
Someday when I sit fishing by a lonely river with you Mehr, old and grey but still red in the heart, I will be thinking of this favourite playground where I met your mother. She started my journey to become a better man in this city.

Love

Papa

Roxanne Firdos
Bradford, UK

Not the Silk Road

Cobbled stone gives way to dusty heat. Brooding dark Victorian terraced houses conspire no more. The formidable desert beckons. Your elderly father holds your tiny hand whilst you stare into the wilderness. Oak holds China.

Yorkshire to Pakistan: a road trip. In two weeks, you almost die – the car skids the mountain edge.

Your destination a distant dream – a mirage. Perhaps, this is why you call your second daughter by this name or, maybe, your husband chooses it. You would have called her Elizabeth, like the Queen.

Jerina – soon to be known as Zerina. Your father's name is Ram Narayan, but he is known as Sheikh Ayatollah. Your mother's name is Amelia Fowler, but she will become Amelia Williams. Your husband to be - Firdos - we shall all share this name.

Without a visa 'uncle' your driver, flees in fear. Grandfather negotiates with the Police. He is shovelling coal into the furnace of the merchant ships like he did before he arrived in England and married your mother. You notice the large holes in his ears on the journey back to Turkey. You will soon be wearing earnings of gold on your wedding day.

Babylon. The Hindu Kush. The Indus. Soon Peshawar. Finally the Village. 1966.

You will be a dust child rather than a flower child. You will not return home until 1974 - disco and platform shoes await your return. You hold my sisters' hands and board the plane. China holds glass.

Arun Ganapathy
Delhi, India

Journey in Search of HIM on a Summer's Evening

One summer's evening I set out into the fields
near my house in search of HIM
I followed the Sun and watched it turned orange
and pink
And light the world unseen,
Was HE not there?

I saw a White stork
Fly slowly up the river.
Gracefully she flapped her wings
And flew without care!
I followed her for a moment and thought
Was HE not there?

Then I saw a tree in the middle of a field,
I watched it from afar
Its leaves danced in the wind,
They danced and they danced,
Was HE not there?

Then a hut near the tree,
Thatched and so tempting,
Inviting me in
Inside it is empty
And cool and shady.

I lay down to rest
My journey has ended

An hour passed
Now all was still,
Only a HEARTBEAT
HE, is HERE

Farah Ghuznavi
Bangladesh

The Homecoming

In the end, the goat broke the dam. He was ripping out the spiky blades of grass thrusting valiantly through the cracked mosaic floor. My father had lovingly supervised the laying of that diamond-shaped pattern just a few years – and an eternity – ago, laughingly pretending deafness at my mother's exasperated entreaties to come eat.

Now, it resembled the uneven fragments of a jigsaw, scattered by the destructive force of a childish hand; a reflection of the carnage visited upon our once-serene lives.

With the arrival of the Pakistanis in early 1971, we learned to sleep lightly, whispers of the devastation elsewhere travelling on the south wind even to our backwaters. So, when known supporters of Bangladesh - along with Hindus and young girls - began disappearing after being taken to the military camp for "routine questioning", we did what we had to.

My father's decision to shelter the freedom-fighters triggered the conflagration that ultimately destroyed our home. I wasn't around to watch it, my sisters and I sent away to safety. A terrified adolescent, I kept my promise to him never to display weakness.

Until I returned to meet the lonely figure of my dignified mother, still standing amidst the ruins of a life; and visited the grave of a man who had suffered such torment for doing the right thing. Only now, staring at that shattered mosaic, could I allow my flash-frozen tears to melt away, bringing the chill, healing emptiness of a relief long-withheld...

Atar Hadari
Hebden Bridge, UK

The Return

You dreamed one of our children died
and came back to console the other –
not us, that would have been beyond even her gift
but for her sister, who would have been spared
the crying for a moment, seeing her face
that would have started every day
with the cry of her name, as now, then inconsolably
wept.

How we would have fared
I don't know, is not worth asking
though the tears at the thought
are just the start, there is no knowing where it ends
but if you ever know how
the taste of that cake lingers
in the back of your throat, slow
and so dry to force into your heart

you let me know, I'll be
beyond tears, beyond dreaming
all I'll know is, if she goes
I will have gone with her, into the sleep

that no-one wakes from
no-one interrupts for drinking
and when you ask me to wake up
I will stare and see no-one
only her face in the dark
and her hand reaching for nothing.

Sabah Hadi
London, UK

One Day

One day

I have travelled to places
a nomad – here and there
places in a picture book,
some the stuff of dreams.

A small town
some miles from my city
in the Plateau Deccan
is one place I never wish to go.

I have heard about the place
how real could it be?
It is, they say – all of them
and I still have not been there.

Will this place be a step backwards or
will there be ghosts there, I may never overcome
in lifetime this or more?
Will I come back with eyes sore?

All these years, I have waited
but no one has told me
neither my friend nor foe
but I know one who will speak.

Who will take me there,
where my father lived
half his life and then came out
so we could live ours.

Judith Huang
Perth, Australia

Atomicae

I sat in a ship once. I puked –
it was swaying Singapore
and Tioman. I was birthed
in a dark land I never saw
born, I was walled in a balloon.
I am a small girl in a carton
shipped from Canton to Cantab,
New England. Before me sits a puzzle:
Styrofoam provinces of China.
I roll them over my unintelligible
tongue. One day my walls will be sponged
sunsets on orange hills.
the seed pants sea,
furlong, furlong –

I am a stone from fair
where all year the bright orange trees
are song and heat is sky
as the black of my hair.
Is a rose still a rose with two r's?
Always wanted more than my fair
Okinawa, I wanted to go there, the only
space I would allow the inner ear
of my Korean sister. Photographs,
when pasted from long
enough, make a wall of sense,
and many people in them are
long since. I have longed for
for long since.

Coconuts are seeds, although
hollow. The flesh grows
gradually, meets in the middle.
Washed ashore, the seed suns
in air. Waters rise, waters fall,
they build a wall out of buried sand
and before you know, trees.
I would live in such a bowl.
Coconut water, sweet, has its own tides.

Skinder Hundal
Birmingham,UK

Ancient Clouds

Disguised almond eyes under the fog of a spectacle

Transcending energies like a matrix tentacle

Piercing beauty like an abstract shimmer

A smile and embrace a 'jaadu' forever

An infinite soul from an ancient time reconnected in Chicago

... the feeling is sublime.

Salahdin Imam
Dhaka, Bangladesh

Australia Dreaming

From Sydney, sophisticated, cosmopolitan, scenic, we fly in one giant hop of the Qantas Kangaroo – over hours of steadily more barren land – to Alice Springs. Emerging shakily from the plane we see this is now a different zone, a different time: no blue dome can be as achingly high, as 360 degrees empty as the Sky in the Australian Bigness, no Sun more buzzing with alien intensity. Alice Springs has motels, cafes and swimming pools but it is clearly the White man's last outpost, situated on the edge of the Sacred Territory, and it is here that I first see them, in mixed groups, now shuffling, now sitting silently under ragged trees, caked in dust like a sadhu's ashes, the Aborigines. There is something about their manner that I can't quite place till it finally clicks: they are Heavily Waiting, for what, since when, for whom, why, no one can tell.

From Alice Springs it is another 5 hours of hypnotic driving into the deep interior, the geographical centre of the Australian continent, the Red Desert, where iron oxides in the soil cause it to rust! The effect is startling as the land starts turning warm, vibrant red. Exactly in the center of the Red Desert, in the middle of the middle, stands the Great Red Rock, Uluru, rippling with magnetic charm, the holy Mother-Snake of the Aborigine people, the valiant force of a religion 40,000 years old. Yes, they are Waiting-because they know they will finally outlast us all.

Sahna Iqbal
Birmingham, UK

Desired Flavour

Breathing it in as I walk through the narrow streets
Ripped posters of bollywood, Baba smoking a huqa in the corner
Blazing hot sun heating up under my salwar suit
Gold diamonds with a string of lace sequins on my shoes
Blisters pop as I hop; loosen my scarf around my neck
Sukhi from Southall winks at us as he see's us walk in
Doesn't this remind you of something? Himalaya theatres showing of Devdas
Intense colours, dreamy sceneries; mountains, rivers, the night life, spice life, dream light
Henna patterns glistening in the sun as they dry
Mothers left on the street to cry bidding their daughters goodbye
Got those married off to a fresh man from Punjab.
Walking by Simla's the sarees call me
Bottle green, intricate embroidery, beads dazzling crazily
Soho Road the next place to be
Chandni chowk's mango lassi, pistachio barfi
Adds a beauty to the mouth
But what is a Jalebi without a sugar coat?
That sweet taste gone wrong
The desired flavour smashes in your heart
Wish you could dream of touching your senses
Again and again
As they sizzle away from you goodnight

Farrah Jarral
London, UK

Pilgrimage

They welcomed me with a steel tumbler of fresh buffalo's milk, the taste at once strange and yet familiar. The dusty, ochre, half-baked road took me through clouds of smells I perhaps once detected in clotted air among the folds of the dupatta of a visiting aunt long ago. Eucalyptus trees and orange groves shaded our path to a tiny hamlet near the river Jhelum, many miles from my plane's touchdown on Pakistani ground. The river, one of the five arteries of the Punjab, once flowed clear and cool with river terrapins and fish in abundance, they say. My aunts and uncles swam here as children before their transplantation to English soil. Bright green swatches of wheatfield swept past, ripe with sap and ribboned with discarded plastic bags, dubious flags of modernity. Behind one such field was my grandfather's modest rectangular plot. The low perimeter wall encompassed a little local school he ran, teaching barefoot urchins their alif bey. Next to this, his tiny garden sprouted chillies, corn, coriander and tomatoes under golden sunshine. An open Quran lay open on the table, cursive script flowing across the creamy pages flickering in the breeze. I bathed from a bucket of water and wore cotton clothes made for me, awaiting my arrival. I recognised that chair, that jug, from photographs sent over years. Love, reverence, gratitude, homage – all poured forth on this, my first pilgrimage. But home will always be my English seaside town, complete with seagulls and chips, and salty air.

Pravin Jeyaraj
Sutton, UK

Coffee with a Stranger

I sipped the cappuccino as I looked out of the window of the coffee shop. I could not stop thinking about what happened.

"Excuse me," a voice penetrated my thoughts. I looked up. Standing on the other side of the table was a man I had not seen before, blonde hair, apparently in his thirties and dressed in a grey suit, white shirt."Is it ok if I sit here?"

I looked around the coffee shop. There was no-one else here, except the baristas and the manager. There were plenty of empty tables. I was not in the mood for my space to be invaded, but to say no would be just rude.

"Ok," I replied reluctantly, hoping that he would take the hint. He did not. I took another sip of my cappuccino and continued to gaze out of the window.

"So, how did you get here?" the man asked.

"Not that it's any of your business but I happened to be in the area."

"I mean, how did you get to this point in your life?"

"Look, mate. I don't see why I should tell my life story to a complete stranger."

The man seemed non-puzzled at my indignation. "Tim, I may be a stranger to you but you're not a stranger to me. I've known you since the beginning."

"Oh really," I replied incredulously. "So perhaps you can tell me how I got to this point?"

"Sure. Can I get you another coffee?"

Adrian Johnson
Birmingham, UK

Impshi, impshi! Jaldi, jaldi!

"Thirty seven years old again," she said with a twinkle in her eyes. Sometimes I believed her. But I am forty now and can do the maths. On her birthday granddad used to bring a steaming, dented, silver dutchie full of spiced, pungent, curry, smells of cumin, chilli and cardamom seeds to carry her back, back to Lucknow, 1947, heat, ten years old, hockey with the locals, army child adventures, magic, murder, another country.
Simply, everything changes.
"We'll take a short trip up the road, your favourite restaurant, for lunch, for your birthday."
"Impshi, impshi. Jaldi, jaldi!" I add as she always did to me as her little boy.
Back home. Safe, familiar. Family and feast, ahead.
"Can you push, son?" Mum craned her neck round.
Huge rubber wheels and silver footplates. It was my turn to push her, up the hill. Tuck blankets round her legs and walk on. Past boyhood, skip past school gates and her outstretched hands and smile, wheeling towards today's party and presents.
At the crossing a two inch curb troubled me, but not mum.
"There's no break for the chair!"
I'm clumsy and she could tip forward, into traffic, as it whooshes past.
"Come on son, push it up and shove it. I've learned to walk three times you know - steamed through death on each side of the track, from east to west in the heat of India, towards nothing but an idea and new Pakistan. "
"You're not nervous, are you now, son?"
"Impshi, impshi, jaldi, jaldi!" she whispers and smiles.
We walk and roll on with India rubber, heat of Lucknow and love – all around.

Rasagya Kabra
Ghaziabad, UP, India

The River

The river flows. Constantly originating from the fatherly glacier and meeting the ever accepting sea. In the course of her journey, she sustains all sorts of plants and animals. Her environs need her. She is the elixir of their life. She touches their life only to enrich it with that of her own. Her association with them is only momentary for she goes on, knowing that her own fulfilment lies only in meeting the sea. From the instant she is born she only traverses the distance separating her from the sea.

What will happen if the river loses faith in her ability to meet the sea? Her waters will run wild and will destroy the world which once fed on them. The river will be scattered, her soul and life wasted on useless objects incapable of holding the immensity of her being.

But the creator instils such superlative a faith about meeting the sea in the soul of a river, that a river never stops flowing. It is maybe to showcase this journey of undeterred faith and allow life to benefit from it that glaciers are never found on seashores.

Rahul Karmakar
Assam, India

The Sea

IT ISN'T easy to see the sea. Not from a hilltop village 1,500 km inside the Indian coastline.

Father Rebello would often tell us how the waves caressed the beach behind his house at Calangute, Goa. How he collected seashells, dipped in the saline waters, rolled on the silvery sand and sun-bathed.

He had promised to take me to his beachfront home. That was before malaria took him to the cemetery behind our house at Mawlynnong in India's Meghalaya state. Friends said I cried the most; I had a reason to – my ticket to the sea lay buried.

I, son of a poor farmer, was 16 then. I had grown up on grandfather's anecdotes – about how his ancestors trekked miles to the Bay of Bengal and returned with cowries and salt. But grandpa wasn't as vivid as Father Rebello.

Partition in 1947 put paid to grandpa's desire to retrace his ancestors' footsteps. The best he could do was gaze at the adjoining plains of Bangladesh from our backyard 600 feet above. "I will see the sea for you," I had promised him.

I kept that promise on my 90th birthday today, the 21st of December 2065. I saw the sea submerging the broomstick plants on our farmland close to the international border 300 feet down the hill.

But why am I shivering, not sweating? And why's the seawater turning to ice? Has Global Freezing set in, as Father Rebello had warned?

Father

FATHER SMILED. But I could sense he was smiling through me.

It was the smile he had smiled when I received him at Varanasi railway station in India's Uttar Pradesh state. He hated travelling out of hometown Guwahati, the capital of Assam. But I had insisted he came to Varanasi for grandfather's *pind-daan* – Hindu ritual to release spirits from worldly attachments – before I was transferred out.

I was never close to father. He was too much of a perfectionist for company. His face always wore a frown and he was short-tempered. We somehow never communicated beyond the formalities. The longest – precisely 11 minutes – we had conversed was the day I left for Varanasi to take up a job.

During the six days he stayed in Varanasi, he was uncharacteristically reticent. "When are you coming home?" he asked after boarding the Guwahati-bound train. "Soon," I replied as the train began to move.

The soonest I could manage a home posting was five years. Father smiled when I stepped through the door. He kept on smiling, and I failed to understand why mother said he was unmanageable. I came to know in 24 hours.

For the next five years until his death, I was closer to father than anyone else. But he never felt it. No one with Alzheimer's does, not yet.

Eisha Karol
London , UK

My Mother

My mother is the source of all the happiness in the world
And of all the sadness
She gave me love like a feathered bird
That sits in my stomach waiting to spread its wings
Keeping quiet I listen to its cooing

My mother is a mango tree whose leaves I want to stroke
I need the fruit to squeeze the juice to feed the bird
My mother is the root inside me
Her branches fuse their stems throughout me
Occasionally producing flowers
That you pick when you say that I am nice

Her absence is like winter;
Or a desolate morning
That sends me all over the world
Trying to touch the tail of the bird

My mother is the chute down which I fell
And smashed into a thousand smithereens
Do you see the pieces of me wandering the earth
Trying to connect with one another?

Tanuja Karunarathne
London, UK

Journey Of So Called Life

When the cold winds blew north
I held your hand lovingly with a torch.
You looked at me once,
And thousand unspoken words flew out.
How far must we go?
How can we carry on with this Journey we began?
When will this war be over?
So you and I can play Mummy and Daddy again.

You held the rifle close to your heart
I held your hand tightly and
You held our child
Like a precious diamond.
I looked up to the sky,
Felt big tears of sadness
Welling up in my eyes.

Dark night with its many secrets,
Holds my dreams in your pockets,
It will light your way, when you think of home.
I will walk back to the village alone,
Without you by my side.

Oh beloved moon, shine bright for me,
Keep us safe till he returns.
Tell my Owl friend to protect my beloved.
I will be waiting to hold you again, in this so called
Journey of life once more.

Masud Khan
Dhaka, Bangladesh

Finding Anjan

"Do you remember me?"
Silence. Just the sound of breathing; a sharp intake of breath, and then more silence.
"No."
I waited for more, a word, a smile; any indication that he knew me, remembered me.
I smiled, tried to convey to him my love for him, my need for him to remember me.
I tried to touch him, hold his hands through the playground gate. He stepped back, fear and something else playing in his eyes. Then the moment was gone; he turned around and ran back to his friends in the schoolyard as the school guard noticed me and moved towards me. I walked away.
That was the first time I saw my son Anjan after almost 5 years; taken away from me by his father when he was just a baby; stolen and hidden away behind a wall of money and power until Anjan turned seven, when my rights of custody ended under Islamic law.
Then, a few months after Anjan's seventh birthday, I found him. After that first meeting outside the school gates, I returned to the school every day. We did not speak; I just stood and smiled at him. After a few days, he returned my smile. After a few weeks, he walked to me again; let me brush his fingers with mine.
"Do you remember me?"
He nods; no fear now, just that something else in his eyes.
The next day he was taken out of school. I will find him again.

Usha Kishore
Isle of Man. UK

The Journey of a Lifetime

Abivadaye Angirasaha Bharadwajagotrothbhavayai...

This is how I introduce myself –
I am a Brahman woman
of the gotra Bharadwaj

My ancestors - high priests
practising Rigveda, doyens
of yagnas, mother worshippers...

I am a woman cloistered
in Brahmanical patriarchy-
A woman not permitted to chant
the Gayatri – the mantra of a woman...

I once drew my breaths in the coast,
where palm fronds echoed my sighs
and frolicking waves chased my
dreams – melting in the moonlight
of monsoon nights, I danced with
serpent gods on enchanted courtyards...

Then I became an eternal wanderer –
I crossed the seas, incurring the
wrath of the clan –
I became an exile –
I lost my language, my
history, my culture...

I am now a bird with many
tongues – I write in English,
I dream in Malayalam, I think
in Hindi - I have no language
of my own...

My culture is now called
diaspora; my writing,
postcolonial –
I don't recognise myself,
anymore –
I am a translated woman -

I sprinkle my days with words,
I bathe in the seven seas of
consciousness -
I begin my mornings with
the Gayatri and Chaucer;
My twilight prayers are
Keats's dreams blended
with Mira bhajans -
I live in an in-between space...

I write my history in poetry -
My poetry is a journey
through the East and
the West; through cultures
that meet and marry,
through languages that
flow in and out of one another...

Sanskrit quote – Sanskrit greeting by Brahmins belonging to the clan/family of Bharadwaja – can be translated as – "I, born into the Bharadwaja clan of the rishis (sage) Bharadwaja and Angirasa, greet you." This greeting is primarily for male members and women do not greet each other this way. However, I have subverted the greeting into Bharadwajagotrothbhavayai (feminine declension of the verb) instead of the traditional Bharadwajagothr othbhavaya (male declension).
Gotra – clan/family
Yagna – sacrificial rite
Rigveda – One of the 4 vedas
Gayatri – a mantra or chant
Bhajan – hymn

Deepa Kylasam Iyer
Puducherry, India

Tryst with Destiny

The haggling pedlars divided
Books, bank-notes and bureaucratic files,
And quickly settled down to the business of
Dividing human piles.

The Faustian Pact drove a human caravan
Of unimaginable proportion.
They clung to each other
Their priceless possessions
A price dropped with each passing mile,
Till they bartered it all away
For nothing in return.

The wailing infant
Is unable to comprehend-
Why his mother's lifeless limbs
Will never pick him up again.
The invalid awaits death
Amidst bloated vulture and ravenous wild-dogs.
The fortunate are in the open graveyard.

The sons of a lesser God,
Who do not fall prey
To the beasts of the jungle
Are preyed upon
By their turbaned brethren,
Who ravish them
And drink their blood in the name of God.
Like droves of cattle
Led kindly to the abattoir,
With the patina of destiny on their faces,
The hapless millions flock towards
A new dream nurtured in penury;
Oblivious to the intransigence of their kings
And their caprice that wrote
The macabre story of two nations
With the sweep of a pen.
By severing the umbilical cord,
Tearing lives apart, burying hopes,
Wiping off smiles
From the faces of millions;
The travesty of justice
Has made peace an unwanted luxury,
And their brothers, eternal refugees.
The odious and grotesque exodus
Is the trek of the uprooted;
A journey of no return.

Hazel Larkin
Co Kildare, Ireland

Party in Mumbai

The chattering lessens as people take stock of our entrance. There is nothing subtle or furtive about it. Uncomfortable, I fiddle with the pallu of my sari, the zari work taut and slippy under my fingers. Naresh is still holding my hand. I make a mental note of this in order to thank him for it later. Almost imperceptibly, he squeezes my fingers and gently draws me further into the hall.

My two children – who are obviously *not* his two children – follow us. Their laughter is excited. They are keen to meet the Birthday Girl.

Naresh propels me across the room to meet the parents and grandmother of the child in whose honour this lavish celebration is.

I make to touch the feet of the grandmother and am stopped and chided by her. Her fingers are surprisingly strong on my shoulders. She greets me with a kiss on my cheek instead; smelling vaguely of incense from her 6 o'clock prayers, Chanel 5 and jasmine hair oil.

After greeting me, she summons up a glass of *Sula* red wine for me. I take a deep draught of the rich, plumy liquid. The faintly spicy flavours of the Marathi grapes flood my mouth.

The offering of the elixir has sealed my acceptance. The room, which I didn't realise was watching, exhales and Naresh brushes my cheek with his lips. The other guests mingle, chatter and dance as the DJ replaces 'Tum Bin' with 'Salaam-e-Ishq'.

Sid Lassi
Birmingham, UK

Puttar! (Child)

'Puttar! Before you jumping, - listen!'
    Long ago, simple old times. - Was farming village; journey to nearest town have to be made to negotiate best deal for entire village's harvest. Three men! Each a witness to the other, simple, true and honest; do journey on foot - hope of all village with them.
    Walking for hours the sun setting; calm temper of the sky vanishing, it raining, - but they continue walking. Wet mud; path become heavier! Sky *puttar* darkening, wind is joining in too; savage storm arriving like unfair lover. Walking impossible!
    Seeing abandoned hut they taking shelter; worried, delay no good!
    Old, wise one, he say *'we sleep, leave minute storm going.'* No sleeping *puttar.*
    Lighting! Keep striking by the hut, all around it.
    Wise one, he saying; *'one is destined to die. We need to rest, god forbid, we arrive late. One by one we go out and stand for awhile; the one that is to die, - well so be his fate '.*
    All silently agreeing. Old one going first; away from the hut he standing, - nothing, he come back in. Second doing same; but nothing. He also coming back into hut.
    Last one! Staring death in face, other two cannot look dear friend in eye. But true to his word, he walk out; seconds pass, nothing. Few more, then. .

    ..Big bang!

Bolt of lightning striking. *Puttar!* - Whole hut blown to bits.
    'No body is knowing what is to come, no body puttar!'

Zhi Xin Lee
Singapore

The Naming of Absences

They didn't use to acknowledge
a lack of something. The world without zeros
was a simple one: what is there
is there. For example, in my basket of fruits
I have two apples and three pears; I will not think,
I have no oranges. The sky is purely blue, not
without clouds; my stomach growls, not because
I haven't eaten, but because I need to eat now.

Possibly it started with a simple urge.
Someone wanted chicken but there was only beef.
The craving grew, its fingers of black clouds
creeping over the horizon. People started noticing
what wasn't there: light, when it was dark;
heat, when it wasn't summer. Specific presences.
The existence of four children
not making up for the death of the fifth.
It was hard to explain this remembering,
this difference. One day they discovered
a puddle on their floor, looked up
to see the circle-shaped sky.
Their fingers traced the shape,
called it *zero*. Many more names sprouted:
a hole; a void; loss. At last
they put a finger to their hearts,
named the feeling
missing.

Mina Maisuria
Loughton, UK

Farishta (Angel)

A house in the East End of London, 1952. A little boy is watching Bill and Ben the Flowerpot Men.

I got lost in the smog yesterday, my Bapu sent me to get some fish. The man's hand came out of the smog and gave me a shilling change and the fish. I had my Auntie's old coat on, all the kids at school laugh at it…but no one can see you in the smog. I never saw the last post box like Baa showed me, honest, I kept walking and walking and then I heard this voice. "Do you know where you're going son?" I took the piece of paper out of my pocket. "Oh, you're a long way from Stoke Newington son". Then she, she grabbed my hand, she wasn't scared, not like my friends' mummies who all want to touch my hand, the colour doesn't come off you know. Not my 'Farishta', my angel, we walked all the way home. Baa said I was lucky, not everyone had a Farishta, I told Baa I didn't mind sharing my Farishta with her. Bapu said we were in the land of plenty, six women to one man, especially after the war, all you do is buy them a bag of chips and a Guinness and they're yours. I asked Bapu if that was forever, he said "Only for the night.", so I said, "But Bapu I'm gonna have to buy them chips every night then". My Bapu laughed.

Munize Manzur
Dhaka, Bangladesh

From Zero Point

Jump.
Excuse me?
Jump already.
What's your problem?
You're standing atop the railing of a deserted bridge in the middle of the night. It's pretty obvious. So go ahead. Jump.
What's it to you?
You're holding up the line.
Who am I holding up? You?
Yes, as a matter of fact…now what are you doing? Why are you getting down?
Since you're in such a rush, go ahead.
No, that's okay. Ladies first.
I'm not old fashioned. No need to wait on niceties for me.
Hmm. You're definitely a woman though. Inclined to change your mind at a critical point of no return.
And you're definitely a man. Exemplified by your impatience to rush through the crossroads of life, because you don't want to stop and ask for directions.

Typical of a woman to think there are answers for every question.

Typical of a man to think there aren't.

If you're so sure there are answers, why were you standing on top of that railing?

I was trying to see the big picture.

And, did you?

Didn't get a chance to see much! You interrupted me. So, your turn. Jump.

Excuse me?

Jump already.

You made me lose my moment.

I see.

You do? What?

A coffee shop at the end of the bridge.

Oh. So…want some?

Yeah, might as well…seeing as neither of us is getting anywhere tonight.

We got somewhere.

Where?

A step back from nowhere.

And that's somewhere…

Yes, that's somewhere.

Let's go then.

Of Bags and Baggage

Time to pack my bags and move back. But that implies reverting. And though I may be returning to a country I was in, I'm certainly not returning to the same state.

Because perspectives change during vacation. It's like wearing an old frayed coat. It's not highly fashionable yet it's comfortable. You wonder if the time has come to get a new coat.

Then you wear it on an unfamiliar street. And while you're trying to figure out what all the signs mean, you notice the details of your coat. How the inseam is double-stitched and can take on rough weather. How the elbows are padded with well-worn leather so when you fall you won't graze those vulnerable spots. And by the time you get home, you understand: this coat's a keeper.

People go abroad and buy the latest. Upgrade themselves. For me, vacationing is more about rescaling. Re-calibrating your soul so it doesn't feel tilted. Discover, uncover, recover.

You get lost and find a quaint church. You write verses in your moleskin journal with rhyme but no reason. And you hear voices in your head that thrill you, fill you, scare you, dare you, uplift you.

I've made this journey to a place where I can breathe properly -- exhale stale thoughts, inhale fresh spirit. I've gone the distance so I can draw that much closer to my soul.

Tisa Muhaddes
Dhaka, Bangladesh

In the Womb

My journey began and ended in the womb. The end didn't come with loud bugles heralding doomsday; instead it crept upon me with a quick lethal injection that permanently closed my newly-formed vision. The only sounds embedded in my memory were of my mother's thoughts. You might think it strange I said her thoughts instead of her voice. But in those early days, sounds were garbled, confusing, and distant. But her thoughts were sharp, clear, and profound. I learned to forgive her by listening to her thoughts. I learned the knowledge of my existence came as a shock to her. I learned she was saddened, no; she was broken, when my daddy quietly went away. I heard her thoughts as she prayed to someone upstairs for a solution. I remember her sprouting angry words. Usually those acerbic words would be followed by jolts that permeated through my liquid bubble. I would cry out to her to stop. And then she would start crying, and wouldn't stop for hours. Even then I didn't accept she hated me. She loathed the very idea of me inside her. I was a growing parasite inside her that heralded her failure as a woman, a girlfriend, and as a daughter. I was a mistake that needed disappearing. Nearing the end, before the darkness, I listened hard to her thoughts. But they were the same, venomous and hollow. I was comforted. Everything was usual. And so I had no warning of the end.

Iffat Nawaz
Dhaka, Bangladesh

Three

My first marriage was arranged. He was a big man; impolite honesty would just call him fat. In bed he made sure to remind me of the difference of twelve years between me and him by arranging his humongous tummy right in the middle as he slept on his side with one very hairy leg holding me down. After the third emergency room visit and bleeding through my teeth I left him. He called me a whore.

My second husband was a best friend. I travelled away and to far places with him, Eastern Europe in the dead of winter, scuba diving in the red sea, kayaking down rivers in South America that still felt warm from live volcanoes and their burning-red lava. With him I discovered physical liberation, I learnt how to take nothing for granted, and how to put my happiness first. In between figuring out individualism and night reading lights I lost him to another. I couldn't call him a whore.

My third marriage was rushed, it was intimate, it made me want children. So we tried and it happened. But my body kept on refusing the new lives; she was still stuck on the liberation and individualism approach. So I prayed, like I used to when I was a child, with naïve optimism and disjointed thoughts. I prayed so I could forget all that I claimed to have known and seen, all that I thought I understood, as a wife, woman and whore.

Sue Newton
Coventry, UK

Pyjama Party

"Mummy, do I have to . . . ?" Parsharan hung her head.

"It'll be fun!" pronounced her mother, buttoning her five-year old into the nightdress and pulling the yoke straight. "There, you look just like Wendy in Never-Never Land." Mrs Matharu looped the red ribbons of the birthday present round the child's wrist.

The invite to the pyjama party had come as a surprise. "How kind of your classmate, Gerard, to think of you!" They got on the pushbike, a 'sit-up and beg' contraption with a child's seat on the back.

Gerard lived in a mansion off Hangman's Mount. As she laboured uphill, Mrs Matharu repeated, between deep breaths, the necessity for 'please', 'thank-you', and 'It was a lovely party'. Parsharan said nothing.

Gingerly they pulled the bell, an ornate handle fashioned in the shape of a snarling beast. The door swung open. From within the house came the shrieking mêlée of unattended children. The mother ambled out, wine glass poised. "Gerard, sweet-ie!" she called.

The small boy, in Batman Joker pyjamas, darted out, wrenched at the girl's wrist, ran off with the present, and left the ribbons dangling. "Mummy, don't leave me!" Parsharan's pink cheeks were streaked with tears.

Mrs Matharu scooped her daughter up from the doorstep and secured her in the safety seat. They whooshed down the great hill, freewheeling all the way, the wind turning the ribbons into dancing streamers. Parsharan giggled with delight. Mrs Matharu said nothing.

Aayush Niroula
Lalitpur, Nepal

Home By Way Of Genes

Tea leaves soak up the early morning mist
as I walk up the soft mudded incline
trying to keep up with my cousins' habituated legs
and as they describe the relations between
the number of leaves on the bud of a plant,
the corresponding taste it carries,
and the grade expert machines at the tea factory grant.

Rounding up a turn,
stands a grand old tree.
Professing of age and stories within.
But I know none of it
Neither can I climb its length
sliding down its barks embarrassingly once upon
grinding against my abdomen.

They eloquently wash the cow's udders,
lubricating it with yellow oil,
drawing out milk into a tin bucket,
and leaving some by experience for the restless calf.
And as I try to pat its bony back,
it jostles with precarious apprehension,
turning to me with a stranger's eyes.

This place I call home,
and this place that calls me a visitor.
Probably because I cannot walk without falling,
clumsily feeling around for rough edges,
on its narrow slippery paths at night,
no matter how much I admire,
its silence splashed on the moon light.

Like an old love I might visit,
to whom I haven't professed so,
as I am without words to explain why
or how or when,
to tell her as such and take a firm stance.
And so year after year I look at her with intimate eyes
and she smiles back to humour an old acquaintance.

Saira Nisa
Birmingham, UK

Universal Time Traveller

This journey started long ago
Before my soul could remember
A heartbeat…

I set out early one morning quite late in my life
To discover the roots from which I stem
Leaving Birmingham for East Africa
Crossing waters, crossing borders, crossing times,
Leaving behind
My memories,
And all of them.

Salt from the sea saturated the fresh breath of the air
Waves sang odes of sea travellers who once sailed across there.
Desert sand quenched my thirst for heat never before felt
Parched lands I wandered, through jungles, wet earth I could smell.

Mountains hid my path, sweet sugar canes enticed me
Heading across north-east, another land, to a time
remembering Ghandi.
Protesting peace to warring men
Our forefathers, all of them.
I've heard this tale, it rings inside forever
Time and time and time again.

Majestic realm, absolute Kings
Palaces where fantasies stark stem from walls therein
Enchanted back across Eurasia to Arabian Spain
Plethora of zestful colours, impale the southern plane.

Transported into Arabian nights
Warm dust colours my skin
Pacified angelic echoes of the call to prayer
Call to me and my brethren.

Bowing down
I travelled through the earth
My feet embedded within the ground
From whence I came, I now return
Not beneath a muddy mound

Uplifted spirit that I am
I soar into the light
I remember now this used to be my original home

And now it is, once again, for life.

Avishek Parui
West Bengal, India

If on a Winter's Night 2 Travellers....

As the full blue-moon rose
through the branches
of the old fig-tree
at the corner of the street
where the tired feet
 were walking back
across the weary city-beats,
I saw you, in the dark
waiting for a hope, or me, or both...
And as we began to walk together,
through the jostling sellers on the pavement
we walked into a star-lit maze
entering the little lanes
where you showed me the old houses
 that spoke of fragrant feelings
 swirling across a song
sung many full-moons back

before the shopping malls were born...

   And, as you talked,
   showed me an old curio shop,
   I half-noticed how,
   we walked past a temple
   just a broken building now...
    I drank in the feelings that hang
   beneath the dim street lamp
   and the old Juliet-balcony
   that still somehow stands...
   An old Kolkata with its musty smell
   Poured out as from a blue wish-well
   The merry music of life...
   Singing in... swirling in...
   Till we reached the sighs
   Till we reached where time now runs
   Till we said goodbyes...

Sahera Parveen
Small Heath, UK

God in Silence

The crowded minivan sped over the dusty gravel road and headed towards the Jerusalem checkpoint. We unloaded and waited for passports and identity cards to be inspected. One man didn't have the correct permit to enter Jerusalem and was turned back. 'My mother's in hospital' he said. But he was ignored. Dismayed, he spoke with feverish anxiety in Arabic to the young soldier who just looked over his head.

We sped the remainder of the way through sepia lit tunnels before pulling into the heady smoke and noise filled roads of the Damascus gate bus station. I whispered thanks to the driver and walked in an almost hypnotic state towards the gates of the old city.

I clutched at the prayer in the pocket of my jelbab, the prayer nervously noted down from an email my brother in law had sent from England.

Colour rushed to my cheeks as I remembered asking him to send instructions on how to pray the tarawih namaaz. It had been so long I'd forgotten.

My mother's words echoed in my head 'namaaz namaaz namaaz, it's the most important proclamation of faith' she'd be so angry if she knew. 'Sabah!' I heard my friend Fiddah's voice behind me and turned to hug her in relief.

We sat amongst the women in the crowded courtyard of the Masjid Qubbat As-Sakrah, or the dome of the rock. I took a deep breath, preparing to pray for the first time in ten years.

As I put my forehead to the consecrated ground during the first Sajdah, and felt the balmy heat of the September evening in the holy month of Ramadhan on my temple, I listened.

And in the instant between the muezzin calling jamaat and the women murmuring feverish tasbih, there was a perfect, blissful and complete silence.

I felt God near and closed my eyes to embrace the moment.

Sonali Pattnaik
Mumbai, India

Rerouting To Arrival

Like on the day I left
I got lost in the departure terminal
and soon after in the contents of the plane
and you wept
as the rains came and went
their load-shed.

I had substituted the objects of my suitcase on arrival:
they were-
your spindly legs, a schizo friend,
who walked in the rain, sucking on
dripping tubes of black ice-
seeking you out to hide with
an international school and bored, diasporic
adolescence.
Also the wide humid and wintry streets of Cairo
dotted with an open admission
of a people's love of their beef.
Its charming contradictions cloaking my
weary feet.

Lost in uncoded hieroglyphics of memories
you sat coded.
And you wept
as the riots came and went
after a broken old monument
testified silently to
a mob's meticulous madness shed.

As I flew across on the same sky on the day that I left
if perchance bored with formal education
you had stuck your head out for air
I was there
hovering above,
circling in the grasp of discovery and unreason
awaiting
a landing.

And many peregrinations past
I thought as for roots, I had shed my last;
So my utter surprise when I
crashed
right at the centre
of your heart's helipad
and on finding myself at departure
I learnt that I had never left.

Amendra Pokharel
Biratnagar, Nepal

From Slingshot Days

I shot to fame, among vagrants, when I shot a bird. That was my first, and the last, day in limelight, at least in the circle of slingshot wielding vagrants.

I grew up admiring birds. I don't know how or when I acquired fondness for shooting them. But killing just one bird made me realize this was something I would never do again ever and would not enjoy a bit seeing anyone do it.

How can shooting birds be anyone's favourite past time?

Most bird-shooters gave no reason at all, inviting my anguish and contempt. Some said, "For fun!" I gave them a questioning stare, the type you give when unconvinced. After a while, showing a little disdain, they said, "What? Just for fun. What?"

Their shifty eyes, quivering voice and face ridden with guilt betrayed the truth. The same emotion besieged me on the day when I was in limelight for shooting down a bird.

I watched the little *fella* ebb towards a different world. Its body cringed with fear, feathers ruffled-up by the unbearable pain that shot through its body. The translucent film of eyelid drooped over its moaning eyes, gleaming with life just a little while ago.

Despite what bird-shooters said, I concluded then, shooting birds is no fun.

Hearing them chirp, twitter, squeak, trill, warble, crow, sing is fun.

Seeing them gawk, pry, steal, peck, rustle, jump, flit, fly is fun.

Watching them slump into lifelessness on the ground isn't funny.

Hema Raman
Chennai, India

Lost Messages

I opened my lunch box and quickly shut it. Those around me wrinkled their noses in distaste and talked just a bit louder to hide their embarrassment.

Once, lunch time meant a few snatched minutes, thinking of my lovely wife in the midst of a busy office day. I enjoyed the aesthetically packed scrumptious messages that she sent. I can even go the extent of saying that I came to know my shy wife's moods and wants better through my lunch box contents. When the sweet dish had been shaped almost like a heart or an apple peeled to perfection, I knew I had pleased her. Chilli powder idlis or masala dosas meant she missed home and those evenings I left her alone with her letters. A tasty but light sandwich would make me have my tea at office and buy packed dinner for us. When I arrived with the dinner she would scold me but I saw in her tired eyes, real warmth.

Then the baby was born dead. She had everything planned. The boy/girl names, the knitting and the cotton nappies all done and ready. For three months, I had canteen meals. Then all of a sudden one day, she packed lunch again. No salt, gluey mess, whatever, I always opened the box, desperately waiting for a regular sign until the day the food was spoilt.

That evening, there was a paper on the table weighed down by the wedding ring. My marital journey was over.

Shadow Men

They came back along with the monsoons.
Teak tree blossoms greeted, grey as the sky.
Green snakes slithered on moss walls.

We covered our thatched roofs from
sharp and gentle spells of rain, with bright
yellow plastic sheets that the military
had used and discarded and waited.

Then our men came, one by one
shadows fragmented. Night air rent with
wails and screams for those who did not make it.
Thankgods from wet lips for those who did.

Mine spent the days with the children.
Getting his scars counted, traced upon
by innumerable tiny hands. He even
let them play with his flimsy medals.

I hid his gun in the empty sugar box
and made spicy chicken curry with
lots of soothing coconut milk but he never
 tasted, only swallowed, burped and smiled.

I waited impatiently for the nights.
He was gentle and violent by turns
like the rains, my back wet with tears
as he screamed of unknown places, names.

I was split open, raw, burning,
he slept exhausted, safely beyond dreams.
I watched as sleep and morning sunshine
made him almost human.

Shadows gathered, moved.
even before the monsoons were over.
We wait.......

Mohan Raorane
Mumbai, India

I to Infinite

Journey of infinite births
84 lakhs different species
and now this beautiful birth of human being...

It's only for human beings
but only for very few human beings,
Final destination is Enlightenment
i.e. merging soul into Supreme Soul
like the tiny drop of water
evaporating from the vast ocean
and ultimately dissolving into the same vastness...

This is seven step spiritual journey
taught in Yog and Brahma Vidya.
It's progress of the seven chakras & senses
those correspond to seven colours...

The starting step being Muladhar Chakra
located at Cervix (at the tailbone),
Red colour of smell sense.
The journey begins with grace of God
and guidance of Gurus...

The second step is Swadhisthan Chakra
located at Coccyx,
Orange colour of taste sense.
The third step is Manipur Chakra
located behind the navel,
Yellow colour of visual sense.
The fourth step is Anahat Chakra
located at back of the heart,
Green colour of tactile sense.

The fifth step is Vishudhdhi Chakra
located at back of the throat,
Blue colour of hearing sense.
The sixth step is Aadnya Chakra
located between the eyebrows,
Indigo colour of mind sense.

The final step is Sahastrar Chakra
located at crown of the head,
Violet colour of extra sensory perception.
Enlightenment is achieved, i.e.

Self Actualization is happened,
Self Realization is resulted,
Knowing of oneself is occurred,
From darkness to light,
From Life to Liberation,
From 'Ko Aham?' to 'So Aham!' (in Sanskrit)
From 'Who am I?' to 'I am Infinite!'

Denise Robertson
Birmingham, UK

Journey's End

Your journey: a defiant choosing of a different destiny. Mine: a pleasant run out, destination unimportant. Our paths cross on the hard shoulder of the M40.
Something... a roll of carpet ripped from a roof rack by the flailing air? No. Something else. Wind milling across the bonnet of my car, slamming onto tarmac.
I stop and get out. I see your perfect form, face down, clothed in tight denim, swathe of golden skin between jeans and short jacket. One shoe missing. I see your ripped toenail and a dark red halo seeping from under your mane of shiny black hair. I turn you over and imagine a flicker of life in your brown eyes. Are you breathing? Can I feel your pulse? Difficult to tell. Traffic roars past on the flapping breeze, a world away from the calm of my First Aid class. I bellow to my friend, 'Call 999'. I start to breathe in to your lungs. Your perfume fills my head. We are strangers, suddenly intimate. Others arrive: an ashen faced lorry driver, two doctors; one helps me before asking her colleague to confirm your death, four barristers in transit. 'Stepped in front of the lorry. Clearly suicide.'
The road is closed. Ambulance crew cover you with a blanket.
We tell the police we want your family to know help was at the scene but you died instantly.
The police call. Hindu girl Muslim boyfriend. Her father said, 'She was already dead to us.'

Bal Saini
Birmingham, UK

My Mother's Land

I was only a child
When without even being asked
I ended where I will die.

In winter I still feel the cold
But layers of jumpers and a woolly hat
Was all I needed to see me through
The snow and sleet.

But it was the other cold
The one that lasts every hour of every year
The later years might have shut the mouth
But you can see it in their eyes.

The Final Promise

In the distance I can see the early morning sun glisten as the rays bounce off the golden domes. It was a journey I had to make. A year would not pass without my mother inviting me to come with her and every year there was an excuse. So every year my mother would come here alone.

This year my mother didn't ask and this year I did come with my mother. As I emptied the urn containing her ashes, my tears mingled with the calm waters of the lake surrounding the temple with the golden domes.

I can hear her forgiveness and feel the loneliness she must have felt on her journey alone.

Ujwala Samarth
Pune, India

Curry Sauce:
A Journey To And From The Recipe
That Is India

"Alright, what's *your* recipe, then,
For a standard Indian curry sauce?"

The Englishman from Wapping or one of those places
that always sounds familiar for no good reason,
Self-proclaimed gourmet cook of the
Mine-is-bigger variety,
Owner for-the-season of a Goan beach shack -- Mango
or Toto's or Sunset Lounge --
Folds his arms and sits back,
Lifting his chin at my husband,
The whole effect unfortunately diminished
By his streaky sun-burn,
And the feni sloshing in the whites of his eyes.

The faces at the table turn to my husband,
One of the pink ones getting pinker with embarrassment
and incipient apology,
The others, merely curious.
We brown-faces find ourselves suddenly suspended mid-air
At various points along an arabesque of incredulity
That begins and ends with something called
Indian Curry Sauce.

"My recipe for *Indian curry sauce*? My *recipe* for Indian curry sauce?"
My husband cracks the words viciously on the table:
A mess spills out, embarrassingly small, without even a hint of complexity.
I stare at this slow puddle in silence,
This oozing map of Wapping
Or wherever, with a chilli behind its ear.

And then our mouths open in unison
And we laugh, laugh, laugh,
Wiping tears and hiccupping at
the idiocy
the innocence
the ignorance
the arrogance
Of attempting to measure out this country into
O*ne* recipe,
One *standard* recipe,
Just. One. Recipe.
For Indian
Curry Sauce.

Jayani Senanayake
Kiribathgoda, Sri Lanka

Pimply Faced Teenagers

Boarding the bus, the pimply faced teenagers,
Not a care in this world, laughing, almost hysterical,
Cuddling and cooing, puppy love blooming.
Hand in hand, oily faces glowing.

But what do they know these pimply faced teenagers?

They look up at us, standing straight,
Chic cloths, fat file and an hour running late.
Must be glamorous to go about your day,
Set jaw, full schedule and a frown upon your face.

But what do they know these pimply faced teenagers?

They wish they were us, we wish we were them,
We wish we were each other, oh what I wouldn't give
to get on a bus hand in hand,
jostling and giggling, out of control.

But what do I know, the blank faced pedantic?

Along the road that they journey one day,
Will they wish they were themselves again?
Or else be content in what they've become,
And go on living with their blank faced frowns?

Colonial Residue

The salty breeze composes friezes
On my subconscious wall.
Memories of a salty past. Tropical salty sweat
That beads the upper lip, the brow and dampens the
arm pits.
It was a long time since I travelled
What used to be homeward now merely a mystic exotic
island.
The smell of her skin haunts me
Lighter than the rest, yet darker
Much darker than what I was used to.
She tasted like honey, her cocoa skin sweet-scented
Like coconuts and pineapple. Her luscious gypsy hair,
Cool and tranquil, fragrant like the temple flower.
I wallow in the sensations, her work-roughened hands
Flutter like butterflies upon my skin. She smiles
The dazzling white of the coconut flesh
Contrasting against the humbler shade
of her sun burnt skin.
It has been ages, as I get down from the car,

the gravel crunches under my boots. The village
children gather
to greet the white skinned stranger. I have become
a spectacle.
Among the crowd I see her, the coconut scented woman
She smiles,
the dazzling white of the coconut flesh contrasts,
against the much humbler shade
Of her sun burnt skin.
A stranger peeps from behind, a child,
barely two feet. The little blue-eyed stranger smiles,
the dazzling white of the coconut flesh contrasts,
against a sun burnt skin.
Lighter than the rest, yet darker
Much darker than what I was used to, yet lighter
Than that of his mother
My coconut scented woman.

Bullet Hole in my Memory

Along the A9 I travel
into the Palmyra fronds, the bullet marked walls
of a torn down past.
A forgotten childhood, evenings spent playing hide and seek,
among the decaying gopurams. The white sparkling sand
embraced our feet and the sea breeze
played with well-oiled hair,
bright coloured skirts that fluttered in the breeze,
and strands of jasmine flowers fastened loosely
in long plaits.
We played around the mounds of earth, the burning pyres
where corpses burned. Some were buried.
We played among the scraggly bushes, crept around forsaken lands,
before a fellow playmate lost both his legs
to a landmine that is.
Some got killed, the rest
scattered away in to the distance, like me.
Some were dragged out of homes, to fight and get killed,
branded terrorists. Yes they really were terrifying.
This is the well where my mother used to bathe,
Her long hair flowing down her back, she used to smile
pumping water from the well.

I used to watch,
as she carried pots of water for the cooking,
her hips swaying with the bulk
the pottu on her forehead gleamed blood red
perspiration formed diamonds
in the harsh sunlight.
Only a few yards away, she was found
lying on the ground one warm evening,
Shot in the head. Her mouth
open in a silent scream. Her pottu bled
The parched earth
soaked up the water from the over turned pots.
We did not have taps you see.
This is where I used to live. The blackened walls
lined with bullet holes, crumbling.
Wilderness has taken over
a place which once echoed
with the screeching of young ones
who perished in the fire
which I survived
and lived to tell this tale.
Now that it is over, here I stand,
With a bullet hole in my memory
from where the emotions bleed.
Here I stand
over the debris of a forgotten past,
of memories
bitter sweet.
Returning was a mistake it seems.....
The setting sun casts shadows on the soot-blackened walls
My shadow seems different
To what it used to be.....

Shaheema Shaw
Chennai, India

"Madam, only Rs. 40 to Nowhere, Chennai!"

So, there I was, haggling with the auto-driver over the auto-fare from my house to college. Learning from the experts, I tried to look as shocked as I could, bargained a bit, and then nodded my head solemnly as we settled on an amount. Then I got in, and we were off. Boy, would my mother be proud when I told her how her child had grown up after four years of living in this city.

I poked my head out of the auto and gazed at the vibrant scene before my eyes. Posters covered every inch of the city walls, people crowded around tea-stalls, little girls rushed to school wearing their uniforms and heavy backpacks, and chickens were having a good time running around the chicken-seller.

Suddenly, the auto-driver pulled over to the side, and grunted something unintelligible in Tamil. This was our destination? Who was he kidding?!

"I told you the address! Where is this place?" I shrieked.
"You told me to come here," he shrugged, rather apathetically.
I shook my head furiously. There was some mistake here. The auto-driver spit out a steady stream of paan onto the road, and gave me an icy look.
"Madam, first learn some Tamil, get rid of that accent, and you can get to your destination."

He held out his hand for the money. I forked it over, and stood in the middle of nowhere, as the auto-driver drove off into the sunset. Just like in one of those cowboy westerns.

Sadaf Saaz Siddiqi
Dhaka, Bangladesh

Something Within

We were in Kushtia to hear the *Bauls* singing the soul music of the esoteric philosopher poet Lalon Shah. We had come down from the North; the point where the mighty Ganges enters Bangladesh, and becomes the secular Padma, passing out of the delta web to the Bay of Bengal. As we were early, I took her to Shelaidah, Tagore's ancestral home, primarily to show her the river from the height of the roof. I thought the place itself would hold little interest; she was doing a travel piece on the holy river for a Chinese publisher. A Chinese-American, she had been a red guard before she realized what that meant, and experienced the cultural revolution first-hand as a teenager, working on a farm as menial labour while dreaming of being an engineer (which she became years later in America). In times when scholars were denigrated and books burnt, she hid and read a choice few, worn and dog-eared from years of subterfuge and use. Her treasured translation of a Tagore novel had been discovered and destroyed; the memory buried deep within, jolted rudely out by my casual change of itinerary.

We reached the estate after several hours of meandering through narrow dirt country roads, colourful smiling children, and endless bright green paddies, postcard-like in the late afternoon golden sun. When we saw the structure of the *kuthibari* emerging in front, painted shiny by some well-meaning but tasteless entity, she had tears in her eyes.

At Last

Green paddies stretching
Wide rivers traversed
And am immersed
In *Bangla's* country air
And I dare
To feel that for which I long
As within me rings the song
Of liberation rising up through
Channelling everything I do
Trepidation of digging roots
Wherein came the budding shoots
Of who I am today

Mud village beckoning
Peaceful grove of lushness dense
And I sense
That this is the place
That I have chased

A young girl darts and dashes
Sparkling eyes enchanting smile
Looks like me
Gaze beyond her to see
The old woman of whom I dream
Surrounded by those who seem
Genuine with warmth and happiness
To envelop me within their fold
Connected history not fully told

The past I didn't want to know
About to show
Catches up wherever you go

She puts her hand on my head
Shock of emotion with nothing said
Doa and welcoming arms
Dignified grace with quiet charm
No apparent vestige of hardships fought
No sign of lessons life and death taught
Or the great strength and pain she bore
And the horror and sadness she saw
Just a genuine wish to connect to me
Her long lost grand-daughter from across the seas.

Navkirat Sodhi
New Delhi, India

By and By

Behind a semi circle of gold
That arch like metal
Holds in an urn
The secret of my mother

In it the toil
The purity of pain
Outside of it
Lies alone

Walking through them
Pyres and pyres
Of snow and dust
Endless timeless
None like her
All the same

Tears well up
From nowhere and then
The heart sees it all

The calm the worry
The smile the prayer
The unequal balance

As fingers reach out
To touch her beating heart
The river calls
For only her ashes

Rajan Soni
London, UK

The Smell of Ancestors

I was six when I first smelled my ancestors.

For days Wadimama's aura had been shifting.
She sang more often,
Her voice going higher,
Into the guavas, mangos and jamuns
In whose afternoon shade we played
As the old women lay on charpoys,
Breathing air thick with the salt of the sea and the sweetness of the tropics

Her face practiced modesty,
Her eyes glistening with the light of a million stars
Swirling and tumbling,
Through the myriad soft folds of her cotton sari
Drenching us with the exhilaration
Of the first monsoons

She wove tender, new, expansive spells
As she plucked rotis off the coal fire,
Slipping extra spoonfuls of kheer
Onto our outstretched steel plates
Adding wings
To that rolling spiraling laugh of hers
That always carried me to heaven.

The SS Karanja came in on a holiday
For those who had stayed up
Tidying and cooking one more dish all night
Beyond the temple bells and before the muezzin call
Waiting with clean ears
For the klaxon sound
As it entered Kilindini harbour

 I remember the day grandfather returned
The sand between my toes,
The arches of my feet curled across the roots of the neems
He walked taller, slowly,
With an old cloying smell that defied my senses

Then, as we all sat cross-legged on the stone floor,
Latch by latch, he drew open the tin trunk.
The ancient spirits of my ancestors spewed out
Carrying the smell of India.

Shagorika Talukder
London, UK

Birds Of Paradise

If we were birds of paradise
Full of colours so surreal
We'd spend our days in the skies
And sing to every golden sunrise.

I close my eyes so I can feel
The humid green of the trees
And in my mind it seems so real
So vivid in its magic appeal.

On my skin I sense a soft breeze
So precious in the heavy heat
Its feather touch tries to ease
The soaring summer degrees.

I inhale a smell so sweet
Of rainbow flowers and plants so rare
Where wood and earth and leaves do meet
To make nature's fragrance complete.

On my tongue I taste the air
Laced with scents of fruits and berries
They hang as gems in sunshine's glare
Their splendour I cannot compare.

And the song this forest carries
Hums and echoes in my heart
A divine tune of mythical fairies
With every hour of day it varies.

Mountains covered in emerald art
Line the horizons of this land
Where they end and where they start
Our eyes cannot tell apart.

So in this paradise do I stand
And watch jewelled birds locked in dance
Whose Eden we can't understand
Whose beauty I long to hold in my hand.

Every imagined touch and glance
Is what my wildest dreams comprise
It would be a lifetime's single chance
To see the birds of paradise.

Shadows On A Wall

We are but shadows on a wall
Dancing through life's crystal hall
Our hopes and dreams light the spark
That stops us fading into the dark.

They say that life will pass you by
One day you're born, one day you'll die
And all the days that lie between
Amount to what this life will mean.

But the day is shorter than we think
Through golden skies the sun will sink;

So take a brush and paint the town
In red and yellow, green and brown;
Go dancing where the night is bright
With a thousand stars tonight.

Read the books and see the paintings
And run through rain as if on wings
Take off the suit and book that flight
To see the world with sheer delight.

And when your soul is set ablaze
By one charmer's compelling ways
Don't stop to think what it could mean
For love is far and few between.

Whilst we're chasing shooting stars
Playing piano and strumming guitars,
We forget that one day we'll all go
Where to, none of us do know.

So take a breath and look around
We walk on truly blessed ground
For without this light, we are all
Nothing but shadows on a wall.

Ephraim Tan
Singapore

Connecting Dots

life is unravelling like an-all-too-long-prose
and being complete is only a beautiful metaphor
of midnight words –

sometimes they flower like purple hope,
snugly sharing the cracks on the pavements
or obscure holes in the water tank,
or just suffocating because of the distance between us.

only then,
can I identify your disinterest
that loosens my tight fingers
and tensed chest

until
this body is nothing more but a fable
for our times. with as much meaning
as a dream that remembers only
those who are dead.

and by coming to journey's end,
I listen to your footsteps –
a music soft and uncertain,
streaming
into the distance like silver dust.

Cliffside

here grasp this,
an extended motion
no thicker
than a forearm
and

hang
on.
by this creamy silver
noun –
a thread dyed tight
like a circus rope

strung
over a web
thick with bubbles and
murmuring jellyfish.

hover like an astronaut
over these translucent heads,
and white bodies pulsing.

watch them strip
their earthly skins

and
become
foreign as the day panthalassa*
suspended itself like a silver fruit
on the lips of first men

ripping their mouths apart
and filling
deeply
the fleshy void.

and soon throats will be taut
with sand,
and voices
only sulky
with salt.

*panthalassa (Greek, meaning 'all sea')

Time Always

under the dusty tent
of broken canvas and palm,
speared

under silver leaves
like a paper dollhouse,
they found time.

time always to remember
footsteps that painted the sand
with soft dreams.

mother said there were no more innocent
seconds; none to sate the rasp of the ocean.
but their hungry shovels

had built
little castles of memories. and they liked
to fill the big metal pots mother cooked in

with coral. red tinged and green tipped.
carried them out to the shore in the dark,
when dusk was thrown like a blanket

over the tagua trees.
mother asked why.
did the smudge of night inspire?

yes. they only dreamt more.
pretended that light could be snared
from the falling stars, like coral

bristling with sea magic.

Takbir Uddin
London, UK

Home

My father loved Bangladesh.

In England the cold weather and the harsh rain sent shivers right down to his bones, making them brittle, and his joints would creak in the mornings.

Back in his home the sun would restore his energy and give him a new lease for life.

But this year he did not come back. My father is resting with his kinsman and is at peace with the land he longed for.

I made a journey to his home, a place that is alien to me.

I am lost, confused and embarrassed that I cannot communicate with the people of this land.

They laugh and point as I speak – they call me London saab.

But they are kind and help me through this wet land. The mud feels soft under my feet and the rain is calm and warm. There is no breeze and I long for it.

They take me to my father's resting place. There is no tombstone as nature has left her mark on him as new life grows from the earth he is buried in.

This country is growing on me. Poverty is everywhere yet life goes on. People laugh and smile as they work the land and its water. There is an energy and passion for life. The land grows on you and you become part of it.

As I leave I look back and see it as a land no longer alien to me but as a lost paradise.

Journey to the Motherland

August 11 2009 Abbah passed away in Bangladesh, a country I haven't been to since I was seven.

At 27 years of age, I have to go back to the land that is alien to me, to say goodbye to Abbah.

I'm worried that my Bangla is not good enough, even the man processing my visa is mystified at my ability. He thinks I'm in the wrong queue.

I land. It's muggy, the heat is intense and even the rain can't cool me down.

It takes ages to drive to the village. As we drive I look out. It becomes less alien and more like a forgotten dream.

I arrive and it's my brother who greets me – he's grown up to be the son Abbah wanted.

We talk but I am desperate to see the rest of my family. As soon as I am over the threshold my sisters and Ammah overwhelm me with embraces and tears.

Ammah is upset that I didn't see Abbah before he passed away – I make my way to his grave.

I stand and listen to the prayers, I notice my brother's tears but my eyes are dry. I stand still, bow my head; I am numb.

Abbah came home to the land that he loves, the land that fed him, quenched his thirst. He thought it would give him back his youth.

This is *his* home and I am a stranger in it – I'm his lost son returning to his land to say goodbye.

Richa Wahi
Kolkata, India

The Honeymoon

In

Giant's Causeway

I sit on the lower columns and listen to shrieking tourists compete with seagulls while I challenge the waves that say, "We thirst only for Scottish blood." "Irish Sea, you don't have the guts to swallow an Indian. You won't be able to digest me." My words hardly end when, encased in the shadow of Finn McCool, his reflection falls over the basalt columns. "Let's go. You've wasted enough time already."

Belfast

The group moves slowly, mesmerized by the guide's memorized lecture. I try and lag behind. Unknown faces look at the same ceiling. I look elsewhere. First at a stranger with a striped muffler twitch his mouth. Then at a woman with thick lips and hair on her neck. I turn towards the rock brushing against me. "Look up. That's what you're supposed to be staring at."

Ballycastle

At the pub he drinks Guinness while I sip on loneliness. He talks about us, I listen. He lies, I nod. He turns towards me, and plants poison on my lips. I let it accumulate. He orders another pint, I do the same. Sweat beads crown his forehead. He plays with the ring. But mine is so tight that I can't get it off. He orders another pint, I do the same. When he gets up to leave he is steady. But I'm drunk, on loneliness.

Derry

I smile. Touching a picture of a man beaten, bleeding. I stare past the camera until I see a butterfly, flitter from flower to leaf. Uncertain, but free. It breezes past. And then, suddenly, it's caught. In his hairy hands. I hear it scream. He shows me lifeless, yellow wings. "For your scrap book." My hands grow heavy. "Say cheese", I smile. With a dead butterfly in my palm.

Let's Jog

You've been running
Down a street
Called life.
A busy street
A chaotic street
A maddening street
Where you meet
No one
And you see
Nothing
And you go
Nowhere

It's like standing on a treadmill
And running
And sweating
And aching
But you meet
No one
And you see
Nothing
And you go
Nowhere

Yet you do it
Because you once had a dream
Which
Like a sunbeam
Brightened your life
So you run
And you meet
No one
And you see
Nothing
And you go
Nowhere.

Pass school well
So you don't get hell
Applying at college.
Study commerce
Study MBA
Study bum licking
It'll be more rewarding
When job hunting
Run fast now
But you meet
No one
And you see
Nothing
And you go
Nowhere

Look at matrimonials
Get a pretty wife
Buy a house
Buy a car
Buy some love
And sell your piece of mind
Go blind
To all your needs
Surrender to greed
But move on
And you meet
No one
And you see
Nothing
And you go
Nowhere

Till you figure
That those who were jogging
Are now belonging
To someone
Who jogged with them
But
Because you ran
You overtook the rest
And you met
No one
And you saw
Nothing
And you went
Nowhere.

Acknowledgements

The competition was run in partnership with the British Council.

Sampad would like to thank the following people and organisations who have helped make this book possible:

Writing West Midlands
Birmingham Book Festival
Everyone who entered the competition
All the students who entered the competition from
Garden High School, Kolkata
Sharan Sandhu
Rajiv Nathwani

The Judges:
Jonathan Davidson
Naseem Khan OBE
Sujata Sen

Sampad receives support from Arts Council England and Birmingham City Council.

BRITISH COUNCIL

writing WEST MIDLANDS

BIRMINGHAM BOOK FESTIVAL
READ WRITE THINK

Supported by
ARTS COUNCIL ENGLAND

Birmingham City Council